Collins

AF513307

EXCURSIONS

A course in Social Studies

4 Revised Edition

Authors
Meenakshi Wattal | Debahuti Das

Preface

***Excursions* Revised Edition** is a comprehensive course in Environmental Studies and Social Studies for young learners. This series for classes 1 to 8 is aligned with the guidelines given in the National Education Policy, 2020. Following the curriculum, this series offers a course in Environmental Studies for classes 1 and 2, integrated Social Studies for classes 3, 4 and 5 and separate Geography and History and Civics courses for classes 6, 7 and 8. The series offers features that focus on essential skills to assist learners achieve holistic learning through a multidisciplinary approach.

The Integrated Social Studies course covers a wide range of concepts drawn from History, Civics and Geography. It deals with the study of social relationships and the functioning of society, equipping students with the knowledge and understanding of the past, necessary for coping with the present and planning for the future. It helps students affirm their place in an inclusive society. The engaging content develops social, cultural and analytical skills required to adjust to an increasingly interdependent and interconnected world.

In line with the new syllabus, the series follows a thematic and structured approach. The course material provides activities for cross-curricular linkages to connect learning across subject areas. Based on an interactive pedagogy, the books promote learning through inferential and experiential tasks and stimulating content. The series provides ample scope for the learners to observe, reflect, hone their thinking skills and develop effective communication skills.

About the authors

Meenakshi Wattal, former Vice Principal of The Heritage School, Kolkata, is an eminent educationist with four decades of experience in the field of education. She is an author, an impactful teacher trainer and a resource person who has designed and led transformative workshops.

Debahuti Das of The Heritage School, Kolkata, has a teaching career extending over two decades, and has been a pioneer in evolving innovative methods of teaching. She is a workshop facilitator and always helps children to think out-of-the-box.

Key Features

Varied key features in the series hone learning skills.

- **Learning** – Let's learn about, Key terms, Timeline, In a Nutshell
- **Extended learning and explanation** – Reflect, FactPedia, Figure Out, Weblinks
- **Observation and application** – DIY, Green Earth, World Connect, Geo Connect, Case Study
- **Problem solving and analytical thinking** – Think Box, Life Skills and Values, Picture Study
- **Creativity and happiness** – Enjoy, Game
- **Multidisciplinary and holistic learning** – Across the Boundary, Snap Recap
- **Assessment and practice** – Workout, Test Yourself, Outline maps

The comprehensive teacher's resource materials are aimed at facilitating teaching and assessment. Feedback and suggestions to improve the course further are welcome.

Key Features

Excursions Revised Edition offers features that focus on essential skills to assist learners achieve holistic learning through a multidisciplinary approach. In so doing, the series is aligned with the guidelines given in the National Education Policy, 2020.

Learning

Let's learn about...

- a family
- the different types of families
- working parents

Outlines the learning outcomes of the chapter

Key Terms

- nuclear family
- joint family
- single-parent family
- family responsibility
- homemaker
- sibling
- marriage

Lists the important terms used in the chapter

In a Nutshell

- Early humans looked different from modern humans and were called hominids.
- The hunter-gatherers ate fruits and roots of plants, animal flesh and fish.

Gives a ready reckoner to reinforce learning

Extended Learning and Application

Reflect

Look at weather forecast and answer the questions.

Johannesburg Five Day Forecast

Mon	18-28°C	Sunny
Tue	15-22°C	Patchy light rain in area with thunder
Wed	16-27°C	Sunny
Thu	17-26°C	light rains
Fri	16-23°C	Light rain shower

- Which day is going to be the coldest?
- Which day is going to be the hottest?
- Which are the days suitable to go for a picnic?
- What should you carry if you are going out on Friday?

Includes warm-up tasks to initiate the learners into the topic and relate to it

FactPedia

The study of inscriptions is called epigraphy.

Provides interesting titbits of information

Figure Out

How long do other planets take to complete one revolution around the Sun?

Hones referencing and research skills through small tasks

Weblinks

For more information, visit
https://climatekids.nasa.gov/carbon/

Last accessed on 31/July/2020

Encourages the use of technology for extended learning

Observation and Application

Green Earth

You can stay safe if your environment is clean and safe. Keep your surroundings clean.

Sensitizes learners towards conservation of the environment

DIY

Turn off the lights in your room, and make different shapes with your hands, as shown in the picture. Use a torch to make a shadow of the shape on the wall.

Provides application-based activities for experiential learning

Problem-solving and Analytical Tasks

Think Box

The original copies of the Constitution were written in both English and Hindi. Why do you think it was bilingual?

(HOTS) Facilitates out-of-the-box thinking for curious minds

Picture Study

Look at the picture and answer these questions.

1. Name this building.

Provides exercises for inferential learning

Life Skills and Values

A. In groups of six, write a script for a short skit enacting these characters—sunny, rainy, foggy, snowy, cloudy, and misty.

B. Have you seen how the trees change their appearance in different seasons? Look at this picture and describe the seasons.

Provides real-life situations to skill learners to excel in life

Creativity and Happiness

Enjoy

A. **Be A Weather Forecaster**

In groups of four, make a PowerPoint presentation describing the weather of your country for that day. Present a weather forecast for the coming week.

Addresses well-being and happiness of the students through creative and fun tasks

Provides varied tasks for game-based learning

Multidisciplinary and Holistic Learning

Across the Boundary 2

Read the instructions and draw the route that Magellan and his crew would have taken while circumnavigating the world.

Magellan and his crew sailed from Spain and travelled southwards across the Atlantic, along the coast of South America to reach the Strait of Magellan. Then, they sailed northwards and crossed the Pacific Ocean to reach the Philippines. From here, they travelled along the coast of Africa, across the Indian Ocean. They headed northwards and finally reached Spain in 1522.

Provides varied activities for multidisciplinary learning

Snap Recap

The Snap Recap section contains a collection of mind maps that draw the outline of the concepts you have learned in this book. Mind mapping is a useful technique that helps you learn more effectively and improves the way you record information. They help you see the way pieces of information fit together. Mind maps also help you remember information, as they hold it in a format that your mind finds easy to recall.

Evolution of Human Beings

- Hominids
  - Earliest forms of human beings
  - • big heads, could not stand
- Homo Erectus
  - Early humans could stand uprigh
  - • hold objects
- Homo Sapiens

Provides mind maps for quick learning

Assessment and Practice

Workout

A. Write T for true and F for false.

1. Humans and dinosaurs lived together.

To facilitate assessment

Test Yourself 1

A. Fill in the blanks with the correct answers.

1. The earliest human beings lived in ....
   a. Africa b. Australia
   c. India d. North America
2. The Palaeolithic Age is also known as ....
   a. Old Stone age b. Middle Stone Age
   c. New Stone age d. Early Stone Age
3. .... discovered the sea route to India.
   a. Marco Polo b. Vasco Da Gama
   c. Ferdinand Magellan d. Christopher Columbus
4. A .... is a means of mass communication.
   a. telephone

To facilitate evaluation

Imparts map skill practice

Contents

1 Understanding History

Let's learn about...

- what is history.
- the three major periods of history.
- the sources of history.
- archaeological sources.
- literary sources.
- the need to preserve sources.

Key Terms

- history
- historians
- ancient period
- medieval history
- modern history
- archaeological sources
- monuments
- archaeologist
- literary sources
- inscriptions
- coins
- fossils
- paintings

Reflect

The way humans communicate has changed through the years. How did early humans communicate and how do we communicate today? Explain using the pictures below.

....

....

What is History?

History is the study of the past. History tells us about important events that had once happened. It tells us about many people in the past, what they did, the things they used and the food they ate. We also learn about kings and kingdoms, great wars and battles. History is also an account of events that have happened in the past. A historian is a person who specializes in the study of history.

We study history to learn about the past and understand change. History is full of stories of different people in different times. It also makes us appreciate the rich customs and habits left behind by our ancestors.

Periods of History

History is vast and continuous. Historians have divided it into three parts—ancient history, medieval history and modern history. This makes studying history easier.

FactPedia
The Indian history is divided into three periods—Ancient India, Medieval India and Modern India.

The ancient period starts from the time life began on the Earth. During this time, humans learned to speak, write, grow their own food and build houses.

The medieval period is also known as the Middle Ages. By this time, humans had already begun living in large kingdoms. We learn about great kings and explorers who discovered many unknown parts of the world during this period.

The modern period refers to the history of recent times. This period extends to the present where many new inventions and ideas have changed the world.

Ancient Period

Medieval Period

Modern Period

Sources of History

History, as we know, is the story of the past. But, how do we come to know about it? To learn about your own past, you can look at old photographs and old things you used in the past. You can learn about your parents' past through what they and your grandparents tell you.

ancestor: a person in your family who lived a long time ago

DIY

Find out who you are!! Ask your parents for the following information and fill in the blanks.

Names of your grandparents ....

Names of your parents ....

Your birthday ....

Time of your birth ....

The city where you were born ....

The name of your first school ....

The year you joined your first school ....

Your first teacher's name ....

The name of your first friend ....

Paste your picture when you were in class I

A historian, much like a detective, looks for evidences and clues, and puts them together to understand a series of events. Historians look at many objects used in the past to learn about the people who used them. These objects are called sources of history. Some of the sources give us a very clear picture of the past, while some only give us clues.

Types of Sources

We can broadly divide the sources of history into two types—archaeological sources and literary sources.

Archaeological sources

Archaeology is the study of ancient remains like monuments, buildings, coins, tools, paintings. An archaeologist works at sites to recover objects which may have been lying buried in the ground for a long time.

Monuments: Ancient buildings such as palaces, forts, temples and pillars built by humans are called monuments. They give us information about the society and people of the past.

The Taj Mahal is one such monument which is visited by tourists from all over the world. The Red Fort, Sanchi Stupa, Ashoka Pillar, Jama Masjid and the Qutub Minar are some other important monuments.

Red Fort

Sanchi Stupa

evidences: a sign which shows that something exists or is true; site: a place where something is found

Coins: Coins provide important information about the past. By studying a coin, one gets to know the name of the ruler, the name of the place, the metal available in that place, the date when it was issued and the language used in that region. The study of coins is known as numismatics.

Green Earth

Acid rain, caused by pollution, has brought about the decay of many monuments. For example, the white Taj Mahal is slowly turning yellow. Hence vehicles are not allowed near it.

Inscriptions: are important messages engraved by rulers, on pillars, copper plates, rocks, clay tablets and on the walls of temples or buildings. For example, Ashoka's inscriptions on rocks and pillars describe his achievements, his messages and his religious beliefs.

An inscription

Oral sources of our past

In the ancient times, people did not know any language. They drew pictures of what they saw around them. As they learned to communicate and share ideas through signs, language developed. Information was passed by word of mouth. These are referred to as oral sources of information. Few examples are folklore, stories, songs and poems.

Paintings and sculptures: Paintings and sculptures form an important source for studying our past. One learns about the occupations, dresses and lifestyle of the people at that time. The cave paintings of Bhimbetka depict the life of early humans.

Figure Out

How were punch-marked coins made?

Artefacts: Artefacts including ornaments, tools, pottery, or other objects made by human beings are an important source of information about the time period to which they belong.

FactPedia

The study of inscriptions is called epigraphy.

Fossils: Fossils, the remains of plants and animals usually found in rocks, are also another source of history. Archaeologists use shovels and other tools to excavate fossils.

excavate: the process of digging out buried remains from the past

Literary sources

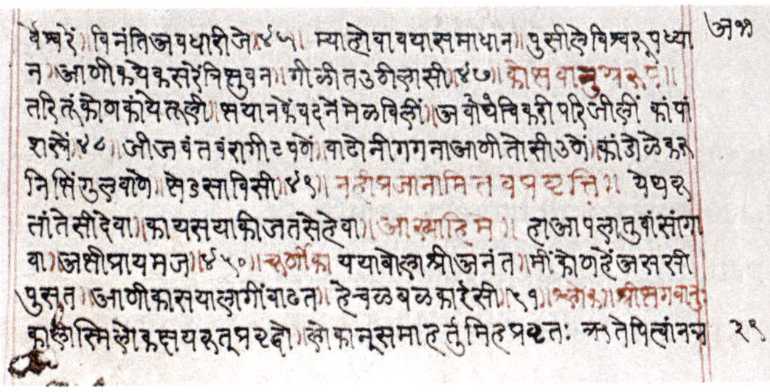

Ancient Indian text

Literary sources are the written records, accounts, fiction and non-fiction writings found by historians. Before the invention of paper, humans wrote on palm leaf or the bark of birch trees which were called manuscripts. These important records of the past tell us about the lives of the people and their kings, their laws and religious beliefs and practices.

Literature of the past were of two kinds—religious and non-religious. Religious literary sources contain stories about gods and goddesses and prayer songs. Some religious sources are the *Vedas*, the *Puranas* and the great epics—*Ramayana* and *Mahabharata*.

The non-religious texts talk about the society, culture, people and rulers of the time. This could be an autobiograbhy by the ruler himself or a biography written by other people on the life story of a ruler. The *Arthashastra* is an example of non-religious literature.

FactPedia
Baburnama is the autobiography of Babur. *Akbarnama* is the biography of Akbar written by Abul Fazl.

Accounts by foriegners, such as Hiuen Tsang, Fa-Hien and Megasthenes left very interesting descriptions of their experiences in India. These accounts tell us not only about the rulers, but also about the lifestyle of the common people.

Preserving Sources of History

It is very important to take care of historical monuments and remains by looking after them and not damaging or spoiling them. Artefacts of historical importance are preserved in museums and are well protected.

Historians and archaeologists work very hard to find out about the past. They both work, hand in hand, to help us learn about the past. Archaeologists excavate sites by digging for buried remains and historians examine these remains and write books about what they have learnt.

Archaeologists at work

archaeologist: people who study the societies and peoples of the past by examining the remains of their buildings, tools, and other objects.

In a Nutshell

- History is the study of the past.
- We can divide history into ancient, medieval and modern periods based on time.
- The two main sources of history are archaeological and literary sources.
- Monuments, buildings, coins, tools and paintings are archaeological sources.
- Inscriptions are text engraved by rulers on pillars, walls, clay tablets and copper plates.
- Religious literature, life stories of kings and accounts written by travellers are literary sources of history.
- We should take care of and preserve our historical sources and sites.

Workout

A. Fill in the blanks with correct answers.

1. The .... is an epic.
   a. *Puranas* b. *Ramayana* c. *Jataka Tales*
2. .... is an autobiography.
   a. *Baburnama* b. *Gitanjali* c. *Akbarnama*
3. The study of coins is known as ....
   a. numismatics b. philately c. cartography
4. The .... is a monument.
   a. Red Fort b. *Mahabharata* c. *Akbarnama*

B. Match the columns.

	Column A		Column B
1.	autobiography	a.	the study of ancient remains
2.	historian	b.	engraved messages
3.	monument	c.	a story of a person's life, written by that person
4.	archaeology	d.	a person who examines sources of history
5.	inscription	e.	an archaeological source to study history

C. Write T for true and F for false.

1. In history we learn only about great people.
2. Any event that happened yesterday is a part of history.
3. We do not have many sources to know about the medieval period.
4. Coins provide important information about the past.

D. Answer these questions in brief.

1. What is history?
2. What are the two sources of history?
3. What are monuments?
4. Name the periods of history.

E. Answer these questions in detail.

1. Why are the sources of history important?
2. What are the oral sources of history?
3. Name two foreigners who visited ancient India. What can we learn from the accounts written by them?

Think Box

In ancient India, some rulers used coins made of gold for trade. What does it tell you about them?

Picture Study

Look at the pictures and answer these questions.

1. What do you think this picture tells us?
2. Who do you think has issued this object?

Life Skills and Values

It is important for us to take care of all the historical sites as they show the great achievements of our past. Write two things that you should not do when you visit monuments or places of historical importance.

Enjoy

A. Know a Monument

In groups of four, collect information about the different types of monuments such as forts, tombs, palaces etc. Collect their pictures and arrange on a chart paper. Write the name of the monument, its location and just one feature of each. Decorate it and display in the class.

B. Make a Fossil

- Take some plasticine or clay or roti dough and shape it into small flat pieces.
- Take items such as shells or leaves or toy animals and press them in the dough, using your fingers. Pull them out after they leave their impression on the dough.
- Keep them out in the sun to dry. Your fossil is ready.
- Organise a fossil exhibition in your classroom using all the fossils you have created.

Weblinks

For more information, visit
https://www.historians.org/about-aha-and-membership/aha-history-and-archives/historical-archives/why-study-history-(1998)
https://knowindia.gov.in/culture-and-heritage/ancient-history.php
Last accessed on 31/July/2020

2 Timelines

Let's learn about...

- the Gregorian calendar.
- the Saka calendar.
- timelines.
- the use of CE and BCE.

Key Terms

- Gregorian calendar
- AD, CE, BC, BCE
- Saka calendar
- leap year
- timeline

Reflect

Look at the calendar and fill in the blanks.

December 2020

S	M	T	W	T	F	S
		1	2	3	4	5
6	7	8	9	10	11	12
13	14	15	16	17	18	19
20	21	22	23	24	25	26
27	28	29	30	31		

1. The last day of 2020 was ....
2. The third Thursday of the month fell on ....
3. The day after Christmas was ....
4. The first day of the next month will be ....

Gregorian Calendar

We use a calendar to know all the days, weeks and months in a year. The Gregorian calendar is the most commonly used calendar all over the world. It is also known as the Western or Christian calendar as it was first used in Europe. It is a solar calendar, based on the time taken by the Earth to complete one revolution around the Sun, which is 365 days. It is divided into twelve months. Eleven of these months have either thirty or thirty-one days; only February has twenty-eight days. After every four years, February has one additional day and that year is called a leap year. Thus, a leap year has 366 days.

Saka Calendar

The Indian national calendar is known as the Saka calendar. In India, we follow the Saka calendar as well as the Gregorian calendar.

The Saka calendar starts seventy-eight years after the Gregorian calendar. Chaitra is the first month of the Saka Calendar. The first day of Chaitra falls on 21/22 of March.

Look at the table given here to learn about the other months of the Saka calendar.

Saka Calendar months	Gregorian Calendar months
1 Chaitra	21/22 March
1 Vaishaka	21 April
1 Jyaishtha	22 May
1 Asadha	22 June
1 Sravana	23 July
1 Bhadra	23 August
1 Ashvina	23 September
1 Kartika	23 October
1 Agrahayana	22 November
1 Pausha	22 December
1 Magha	21 January
1 Phalguna	20 February

Figure Out

India became independent in 1947 as per Gregorian calendar. Which year would it have been in Saka calendar?

Gregorian and Saka Calendar	
Similarities	**Dissimilarities**
▪ Both are solar calendars based on the completion of one revolution of the Earth around the Sun. ▪ There are twelve months in both the calendars. ▪ There are 365 days in a year according to both the calendars. ▪ There are 366 days in a leap year according to both the calendars.	▪ The Gregorian calendar starts with the month of January, but the first month of the Saka calendar is Chaitra, which falls in the month of March in the Gregorian calendar. ▪ The Saka calendar starts seventy-eight years after the Gregorian calendar. Thus, a date in the Saka calendar is always seventy-eight years less than the Gregorian calendar.

Timelines

Timelines are an extremely important source of history since they give us the exact order of various events that happened in the past. In a timeline, the events are arranged starting with the earliest to the latest date.

Look at the timeline given here to show the years following the birth of Jesus Christ, which is marked as zero.

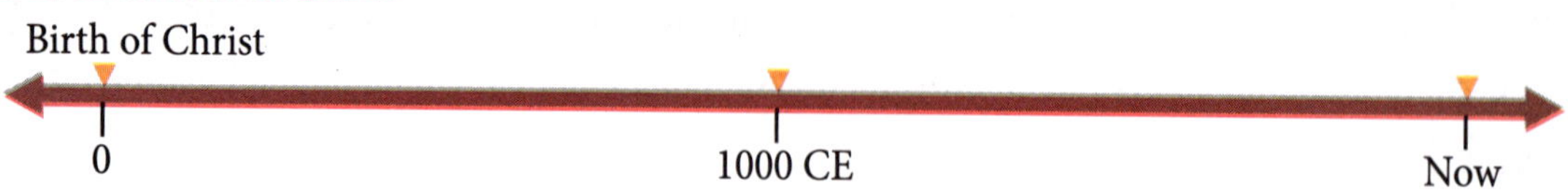

Anno Domini (AD) and Before Christ (BC)

In history, dates are counted from the year of the birth of Jesus Christ. This system of counting was first used in Europe. The year after his birth was written as Anno Domini or AD, which in Latin means 'the year of the Lord'. Historians use Before Christ or BC for the period before Jesus Christ was born.

FactPedia

'0' on a timeline is the year Jesus Christ was born. A century is a period of 100 years. That is why when it is the year 2000, we say it is the beginning of the 21st century.

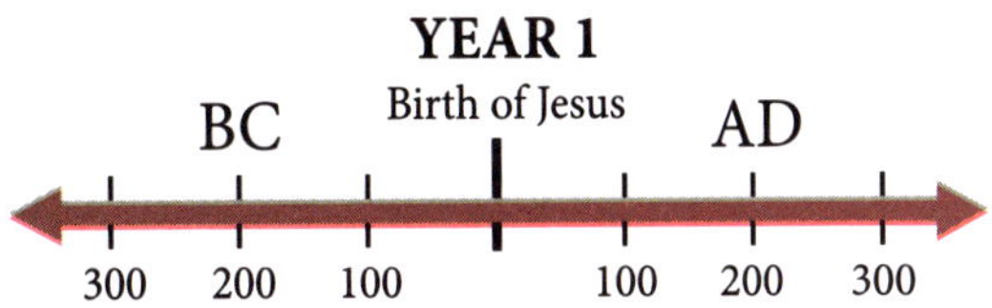

Common Era (CE) and Before Common Era (BCE)

The Gregorian calendar was invented in Europe where the people were mostly Christian. Since the calendar has become so widely used, AD came to be replaced by CE and BC came to be replaced by BCE in order to remove the element of religion. CE stands for Common Era and BCE stands for Before the Common Era.

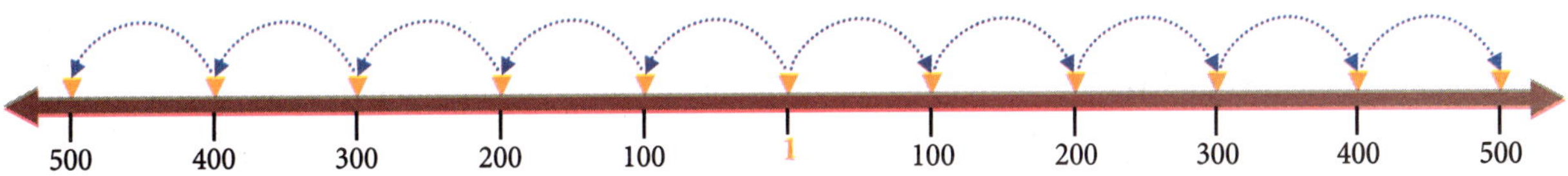

All these years are before the birth of Christ. They are counted backwards and have BCE written after them, such as 100 BCE, 500 BCE, etc.

These years are after the birth of Christ. They are counted forwards and have CE written after them, such as 100 CE, 500 CE, etc.

DIY

Write CE for events that happened during the Common Era and BCE for events that happened Before the Common Era.

• India gained independence.	• Dinosaurs lived on this Earth. ....
• Early humans discovered fire and invented the wheel.	• Mahatma Gandhi was born. ....

Green Earth

Environment Calendar Important Dates

2 February: World Wetlands Day
21 March: World Forestry Day
22 March: World Water Day
23 March: World Meteorological Day
22 April: World Earth Day
5 June: World Environment Day
8 June: World Ocean Day
16 September: World Ozone Day
3 October: World Nature Day

In a Nutshell

- The Gregorian calendar is the most commonly used calendar all over the world.
- The Saka calendar is the Indian national calendar.
- Both the Saka and Gregorian calendars have twelve months of varied lengths.
- A timeline is a list of events in the order they happened.
- The time before the birth of Jesus Christ is referred to as BC or BCE and the time after he was born is referred to as AD or CE.

Workout

A. Fill in the blanks with the correct options.

1. In history, the counting of years began from the time of Jesus Christ's .... (birth/death)
2. A timeline shows us the .... of events. (details/order)
3. The Gregorian calendar was first used in .... (India/Europe)
4. In the Saka Calendar, the first month of the year is .... (January/Chaitra)

B. Arrange the years of the following events on the timeline given below.

- 1869 CE - Mahatma Gandhi was born.
- 1950 CE - India becomes a republic.
- 1556 CE - Akbar becomes the emperor of the Mughal Empire.
- 1700 BCE - The Iron Age began in India.
- 2500 BCE - The Indus Valley Civilization developed around the river Indus.
- 567 BCE - Gautama Buddha was born.

....

C. Answer these questions.

1. What is a timeline?
2. Give two points to show how the Gregorian calendar is similar to and is different from the Saka calendar?
3. Why are the terms CE and BCE important in history?

Think Box

What do you think life would be like if there were no calendars? How will you keep track of birthdays and festivals?

Picture Study

Look at the calendar and answer the questions.

1. Is this a Saka or a Gregorian calendar?
2. Was 2020 a leap year?

February 2020

Sunday	Monday	Tuesday	Wednesday	Thursday	Friday	Saturday
						1
2	3	4	5	6	7	8
9	10	11	12	13	14	15
16	17	18	19	20	21	22
23	24	25	26	27	28	29

Life Skills and Values

Make a timeline

A timeline about your past will show you the year you were born in and the years when the important events of your life happened. These events can be the year you started walking, talking, started going to school and so on. Make a timeline of the important events in your life on a drawing sheet.

Enjoy

Class Birthday Calendar

Form groups in your class according to the months of your birthdays. Put the dates and names in an order, one after the other. Take a big chart and write down all the birthdays as per calendar months and display on the bulletin board so that you never forget each other's birthday. Colour the chart.

Weblinks

For more information, visit
https://community.dur.ac.uk/4schools.resources/History/Timeline.htm#:~:text=The%20years%20are%20numbered%20according,the%20Year%20of%20our%20Lord).
https://time.com/4462775/bc-ad-dating-history/
Last accessed on 31/July/2020

3 Responsibilities of Good Citizens

Let's learn about...

- civics, civic sense and citizens.
- respecting neighbours.
- responsibilities of a good citizen.
- elections and voting.
- caring for public property.

Key Terms

- civics
- citizen
- civic sense
- elections
- election commission
- polling booth
- voters
- public property
- secret ballot

Reflect

Put a tick in the boxes that show right actions and a cross in the boxes that show wrong actions.

Understanding Civics

Civics is a subject that teaches us about how the government of a country works. Every country is run by a government. Some countries are run by kings and queens, while some countries, like ours, are run by a body of leaders elected by us. We learn about citizens' rights and duties from civics. It is important for us to help our government and to make sure it works smoothly. An able government works in the interest of the country and its citizens.

A citizen is a person belonging to a country. We are Indian citizens. All citizens have rights and duties towards their country. To live happily, we must have a sense of respect, duty and responsibility towards each other. This is called civic sense.

Respecting neighbours

To be good citizens, we first have to be good neighbours. Neighbours share the same surroundings, and hence, may have the same problems. People should work together to solve one another's problems and learn the value of being cooperative. Sometimes we only help people whom we know. To be a good neighbour, we should be kind and offer our help to everyone around.

DIY

Are you a good neighbour? Tick the sentences that show you are a good neighbour.

1. I throw sweet wrappers in the dustbin. ☐
2. I play loud music late at night. ☐
3. I let my dog run around in the neighbourhood. ☐
4. I help elderly neighbours carry things to their house. ☐
5. I keep my surroundings clean. ☐
6. I scribble on the neighbourhood walls. ☐

Responsibilities of a Good Citizen

It is important for us to help our government and to make sure it works smoothly as it is in the best interest of the country and the citizens living in it. Let us look at some of the responsibilities of a good citizen.

- Showing respect towards fellow citizens
- Keeping the roads, parks and other such places clean
- Helping and caring for neighbours and elders
- Obeying traffic rules
- Being polite and considerate towards all

Elections

India is a democracy and the people of India choose the leaders who form the government. The method by which the citizens choose their leaders is called an election.

cooperative: to work together; considerate: being careful not to harm others

Elections are held in India every five years. People elect their leaders through voting. All Indian citizens above the age of eighteen are eligible to vote in the elections and are called voters.

> **Figure Out**
> Who is the current Chief Election Commissioner of India?

The candidates who wish to contest the elections, tell people what they would do to help the people and the country, if they are elected. The voters then decide who they should vote for. Every voter in India has a special identity card known as the Voter Identity Card or Voter ID, which has the name, address and a photograph of the person. On the day of the election, voters go to the polling booths carrying their Voter IDs and then vote by a secret ballot, which means no one gets to know whom one is voting for.

As citizens of the country, it is our duty to choose our leaders wisely.

The Election Commission of India plans, organises and conducts the elections in India. It also announces the results of the elections.

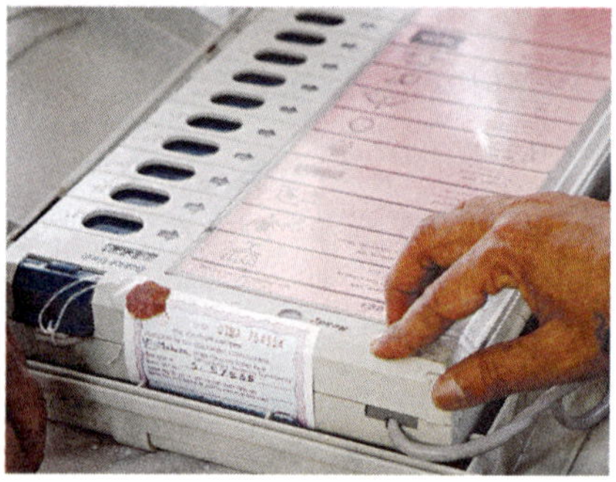

Electronic Voting Machine

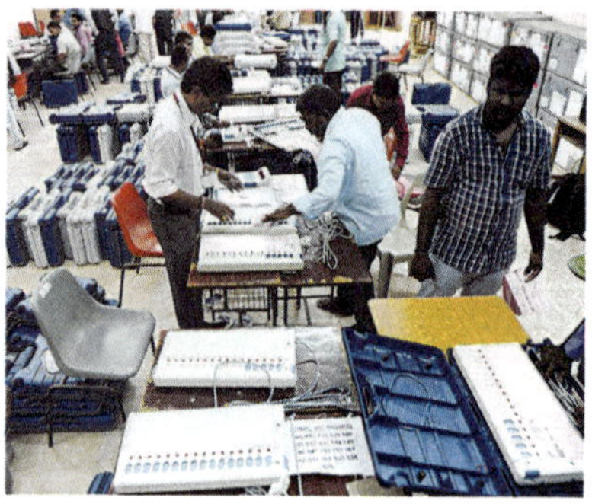

People casting their vote

> **FactPedia**
> In India, an electronic voting machine (EVM) is used for voting. People can cast their votes by pressing the button on the machine.

Importance of voting

Voting is important for all citizens.

- It allows people to choose their leaders.
- If people are unhappy with the current government, they need not elect them in the next election.
- Elected leaders have to serve the people by looking after their needs.
- Every vote is considered to be equal.

Caring for Public Property

Property is something that belongs to an individual or a group. Property can be private or public. Things that belong to an individual or a group for personal use are called private property. For example, your clothes, your shoes, your bed and your toys

candidate: a person seeking or nominated for an election or a job

are your private property. Roads, parks, hospitals, monuments, buses and movie halls belong to each one of us and are called public property.

It is the responsibility of the government to maintain public property. But, it is the duty of the citizens to take care of it and use it properly. While using it, we should obey all the rules. We often go to parks, beaches, gardens or zoos for picnics. We should keep these places clean. Water and electricity should not be wasted. Breaking streetlights, scribbling on the walls of monuments and spitting on the road, all harm the public property and we should never do these things. Looking after public property is a matter of great importance for all citizens.

Green Earth

The environment that surrounds us belongs to all of us. We should take care of it and keep it clean.

In a Nutshell

- A person born in a particular country is called a citizen of that country.
- Civics is a subject that teaches us how the government of a country works.
- As good citizens of India, it is important for us to develop a good civic sense.
- An election is a process by which the citizens choose a leader.
- All Indian citizens above the age of 18 are allowed to participate in the election process.
- The Election Commission of India plans, organises and conducts the elections in India.
- On the day of the election, voters go to the polling booth carrying their Voter ID card, and vote by secret ballot.
- While the government has the responsibility of maintaining public properties, it is the duty of the citizens to take care of them and use them properly.

Workout

A. Fill in the blanks.

1. We are citizens of ....
2. To be good citizens, we first have to be good ....
3. Elections in India take place every .... years.

4. Voters go to the .... to cast their votes.

5. .... means things that belong to an individual.

B. Answer in one word.

1. A subject that teaches us about how the government works ....
2. The process by which citizens choose their leaders ....
3. The minimum voting age of Indian citizens ....
4. The person who competes in an election ....
5. A machine used to cast votes ....

C. Write T for true and F for false.

1. Obeying rules help us to live peacefully. ☐
2. We must only help neighbours whom we know. ☐
3. The government maintains all public property. ☐
4. Every Indian has a voter ID card. ☐
5. All Indian citizens vote by a secret ballot. ☐

D. Answer these questions in brief.

1. Mention two things that a person with good civic sense does.
2. What is a secret ballot?
3. What are the functions of the Election Commission of India.

E. Answer these questions in detail.

1. Write three responsibilities of Indian citizens.
2. What is the difference between public and private property?
3. What are the different ways in which you can help to look after public properties?

Think Box

A. A family has just shifted to your neighbourhood. Write three ways in which you can help them.

B. Why do schools appoint prefects? How are they selected in your school?

Picture Study

Look at the picture and answer the questions.

1. What do you see in the picture?
2. Have you ever seen this mark on your parents' fingers?
3. What do you think this mark signifies?

Life Skills and Values

Community Awareness Programmes

In groups of four, make posters to create civic awareness in your school for the following issues:

- Cleanliness
- Road safety and traffic rules
- Protection of public properties

Enjoy

Class election

Conduct a class election to choose a class monitor.

Select three candidates who will contest in the elections. Each candidate will write their speech. Think and decide which candidate will make the best class monitor. Ask your classmates to vote in the classroom by a secret ballot and then, count the number of votes to find out the winning candidate.

Weblinks

For more information, visit
https://eci.gov.in/mcc/
https://eci.gov.in/about/about-eci/the-functions-electoral-system-of-india-r2/
Last accessed on 31/July/2020

Across the Boundary 1

Values

We always look up to a leader as a role model. Choose a leader whom you admire and mention the reason why you think he/she is the best.

General Awareness

It is important for us to take care of all the historical sites as they represent the great achievements of the past. Write two things that you should not do when you visit these places.

Letter Writing

Writing letters to the editor of a newspaper not only helps you to voice your opinion, but also brings issues to public attention. Write a letter to the editor of the local newspaper about the need for a park in your area.

Language

You are going to stand as a contestant in an election. Prepare a speech stating why you would make a good leader. Remember, the promises you make should be fulfilled by you.

Make Memories

Do you believe that family albums are an important source of history of your family? Make an album of all the old photographs that you can collect and show how the things used then are different from the things that we use today.

4 Motions of the Earth

Let's learn about...

- the concept of axis.
- rotation and the formation of day and night.
- revolution and change in seasons.

Key Terms

- rotation
- northern hemisphere
- southern hemisphere
- revolution
- axis
- orbit

Reflect

Discuss how the pictures differ from one another. Name one activity that you do at these times.

Daytime

Night

Summer

Winter

When you take a spinning top or a Beyblade® and spin it, you will notice that there is a line at the centre along which the top spins. This line does not actually exist and is an imaginary line. When the top stops spinning, the line disappears.

A spinning top

FactPedia

Earlier, people believed that the Earth was at the centre of the universe and the Sun and all other heavenly bodies, moved around it. People would say the Sun 'rises' and 'sets'. But actually, the Sun stays in its place and it is the Earth that moves from west to east.

Now, take a globe and spin it. You will see that, just like a spinning top, the globe also spins along an imaginary line. You will also notice that the line is not straight like that of the top, but is slightly tilted. Just like the top and the globe, the Earth, too, spins on an imaginary vertical line called the axis. The axis is not straight and is tilted at an angle.

Movements of the Earth

Let us study the two important movements of the Earth—rotation and revolution. Look at the given diagram. You will see that both these movements of the Earth happen at the same time.

Movements of the Earth

Rotation

The Earth spins on its axis from west to east in twenty-four hours. This movement of the Earth is called rotation. The rotation of the Earth causes the formation of day and night. As the Earth moves from the west to the east, the part of the Earth that faces the Sun has day, and the part that faces away from the Sun has night. As the Earth takes twenty-four hours to complete one rotation, we say a day has twenty-four hours consisting of day and night.

Figure Out

Why do you think places in the east get to see the Sun first?

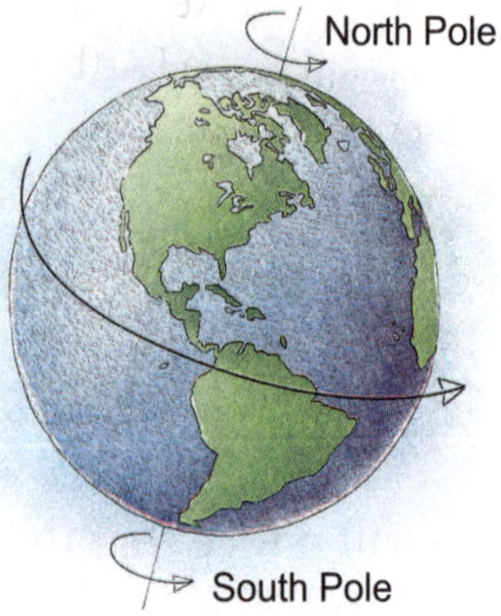

Rotation of the Earth

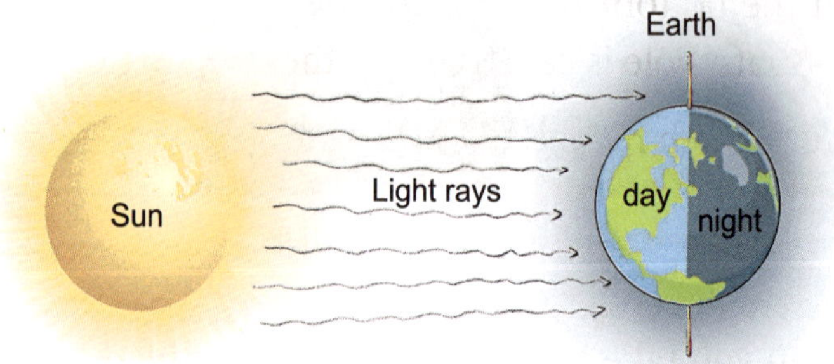

Day and night

DIY

You will need a globe and a torch to do this activity.

- Close all the doors and windows of the room and switch off the lights.
- Now, shine the light from the torch on the globe.
- You will observe that the part of the globe that faces the light is shining bright, while the part of the globe on the other side receives no light and is in darkness. This is how we have day and night on the Earth.

Day and night experiment

Revolution

The Earth not only rotates on its axis, but also moves around the Sun. This movement of the Earth is called revolution. The Earth revolves around the Sun at a speed of 30 kilometres per second. The Earth and other planets move around the Sun in a fixed path called the orbit. It takes 365 days and 6 hours for the Earth to complete one revolution around the Sun. Hence, a year has 365 days. The extra 6 hours, per year, are added every four years to form an extra day in February, which makes a leap year.

Seasons

The revolution of the Earth around the Sun and the tilted axis of the Earth cause the change in seasons. The North Pole is the northernmost point of the Earth, while the South Pole is the southernmost point of the Earth. The equator is an imaginary line running through the centre of the Earth, dividing it into two equal halves called the hemispheres. The top half of the Earth that lies between the equator and the North Pole is called the northern hemisphere, and the bottom half that lies between the equator and the South Pole is called the southern hemisphere.

Figure Out

How long do other planets take to complete one revolution around the Sun?

Green Earth

Too much smoke in the air is making the Earth hotter every year.

As the Earth revolves around the Sun, from April to June, due to the tilt of the Earth, the northern hemisphere of the Earth tilts towards the Sun, while the southern hemisphere moves away from it. The northern hemisphere receives direct rays from the Sun and it has longer hours of sunlight. Hence, the days are longer.

The opposite happens in the southern hemisphere which is tilted away from the Sun. The countries in this region receive slanted rays of the Sun and hence, less hours of sunlight. The days are short and the Sun rises and sets early. Therefore, when it is summer in the northern hemisphere, it is winter in the southern hemisphere.

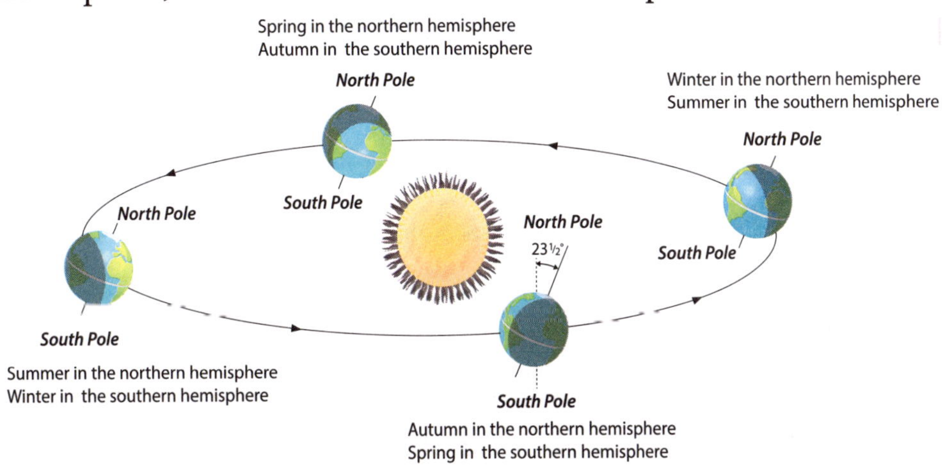

Revolution of the Earth

From November to January, the opposite happens. The northern hemisphere is tilted away from the Sun, while the southern hemisphere is tilted towards it. As a result, the northern hemisphere has winter, while the southern hemisphere has summer. For example, when India, which lies in the northern hemisphere, has summer, Australia, which lies in the southern hemisphere, has winter.

In a Nutshell

- There are two movements of the Earth—rotation and revolution.
- The Earth spins along an imaginary line called the axis.
- The spinning of the Earth on its axis once in twenty-four hours is called rotation.
- The rotation of the Earth causes day and night.
- Revolution is the movement of the Earth in its orbit around the Sun.
- The revolution of the Earth causes a change in seasons.

Workout

A. Fill in the blanks.

1. The Earth rotates from .... to ....
2. The Earth spins on an imaginary vertical line called the ....
3. When the northern hemisphere is tilted away from the Sun, it has ....
4. The Earth takes .... days and .... hours to complete one revolution.

B. Write T for true and F for false.

1. A leap year has 365 days. ☐
2. Rotation and revolution happen at the same time. ☐
3. The Sun revolves around the Earth. ☐
4. When India has summer, Australia has winter. ☐

C. Answer these questions in brief.

1. What is rotation?
2. What is revolution?
3. What is the axis of the Earth?
4. How many hours does the Earth take to complete one rotation?

D. Answer these questions in detail.

1. How are days formed?
2. What causes the change in seasons?
3. What is a leap year and how is it formed?
4. Why does the northern hemisphere have summer when the southern hemisphere has winter?

Think Box

We know that the Sun is also a star. But, why do we see the Sun only in the daytime, and not at night along with the other stars?

Picture Study

Look at the picture and answer these questions.

1. Which movement of the Earth does this picture show?
2. Why does one half of the Earth look dark?

Life Skills and Values

We know that the revolution of the Earth causes seasons. Over the years, climate has been changing in different seasons. How do you think it affects the life of the people across the globe?

Enjoy

A. In groups, make working models to show the two movements of the Earth. Each group must use different materials.

B. Write a poem on the following topics and illustrate them.

- Seasons
- Day or Night

Weblinks

For more information, visit
https://www.nasa.gov/audience/forstudents/k-4/stories/nasa-knows/what-is-earth-k4.html
https://spaceplace.nasa.gov/seasons/en/
Last accessed on 31/July/2020

5 Domains of the Earth

Let's learn about...

- the four domains of the Earth—lithosphere, hydrosphere, atmosphere and biosphere.
- the layers of the Earth.

Key Terms

- crust
- hydrosphere
- evaporation
- water cycle
- mantle
- lithosphere
- condensation
- core
- biosphere

Reflect

Look at the picture and answer these questions.

1. Why is the Earth called the blue planet?
2. How is the Earth different from other planets?
3. What makes life possible on the Earth?

Domains of the Earth

The Earth can be divided into four main domains or areas.

Each domain has its own characteristics and its importance. They are:

- lithosphere
- hydrosphere
- atmosphere
- biosphere

Lithosphere

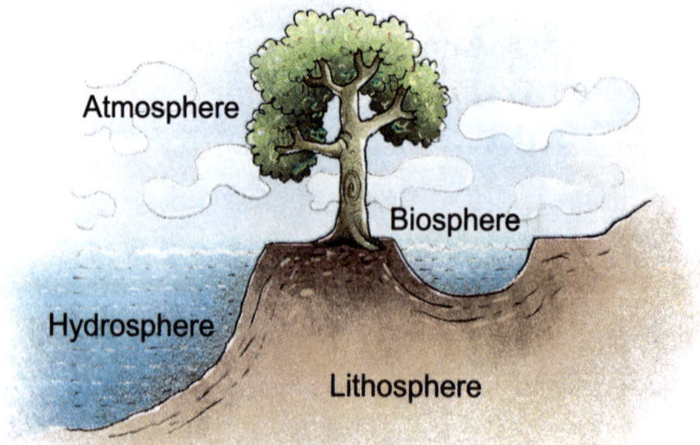

Domains of the Earth

The land masses or solid portions of the Earth form the lithosphere. The Earth is made up of four layers. Its surface on which we live, is called the crust. It is made up of soil, rocks and other solid particles. The layer that lies below the ocean beds and continents is the mantle. This layer is thicker than the crust and is made up of magma. The core is the central part of the lithosphere.

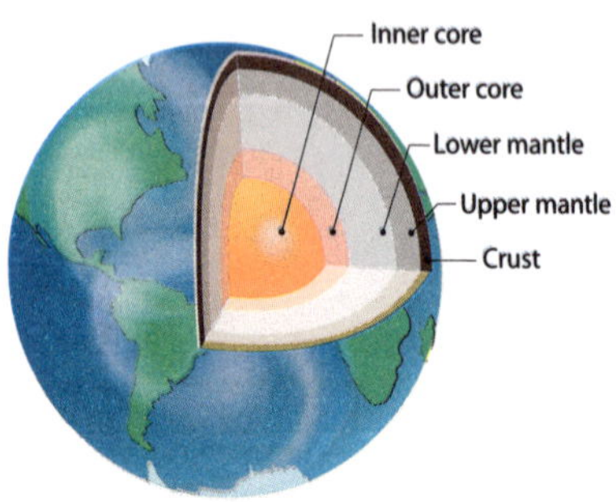

Layers of the Earth

magma: molten rock that is formed in very hot conditions inside the Earth.

It is made up of iron and nickel. The core is divided into two layers—the inner core and the outer core. The core is the hottest part of the Earth.

Figure Out
In which layer of the lithosphere do earthquakes occur?

Hydrosphere

The word 'hydro' means water. Three-fourths of the Earth's surface is covered with water. The hydrosphere consists of all the water bodies found on the surface of the Earth. It includes water bodies, such as oceans, seas, rivers, lakes and ponds. Water is also found below the ground as groundwater in wells and aquifers.

Water exists in all the three states in nature—solid, liquid and gas. The water that we get from seas, oceans, rivers and lakes is in the liquid form. Water as a gas, is seen in nature as fog. When water in nature cools down, it freezes and turns into glaciers, ice caps and icebergs. This is the solid form of water.

Water cycle

The process through which water changes its forms in nature is known as the water cycle.

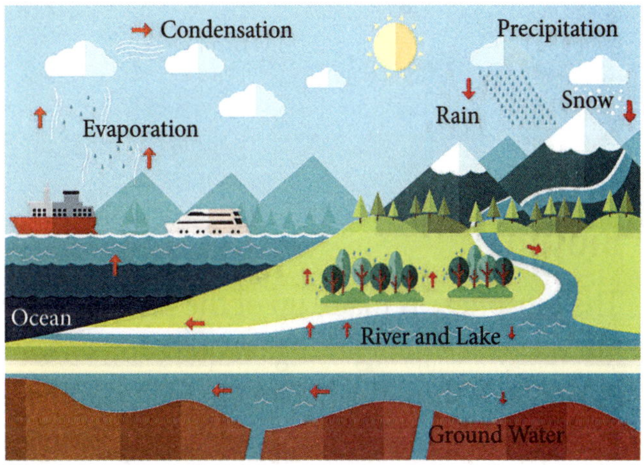

The water cycle

- When the Sun's rays heat up the water in ponds, lakes, rivers, seas and oceans, the water evaporates to form water vapour.
- The water vapour rises and as it comes in contact with cool air, it changes into tiny drops of water and forms clouds. This is called condensation.
- When the clouds become too heavy, the drops of water fall down as rain or snow. This is known as precipitation.

The hydrosphere is important as it supports life on Earth. Water is important for the growth of plants and the cultivation of crops. It is also important for the Earth's favourable climate.

FactPedia
Aeroplane fly in the troposphere, the lowest layer of the atmosphere, nearest to the Earth.

Atmosphere

The layer of air, surrounding the Earth, is called the atmosphere. We may not be able to see the air, but we can feel it when the wind blows or when the leaves rustle. It is

aquifers: a layer of rock or soil that can absorb and hold water; iceberg: an extremely large mass of ice floating in the sea
evaporates: a liquid changing into steam or gas; water vapour: water in the gaseous state; rustle: sound of the leaves moving

the presence of air that makes life possible on Earth. The atmosphere acts as a blanket which takes in the heat of the Sun and stores the warm air, making the Earth liveable for us. It also protects the Earth from the Sun's harmful rays.

The atmosphere is made up of several gases like nitrogen and oxygen, and has traces of hydrogen, carbon dioxide, helium and argon. All of these gases are required by the living things to live. Humans, animals and plants cannot live without oxygen. Plants need the carbon dioxide present in the air to make food.

DIY

Study the diagram and answer these questions.

1. Which is the most common gas found in the atmosphere?
2. Name the gases that make up the atmosphere.

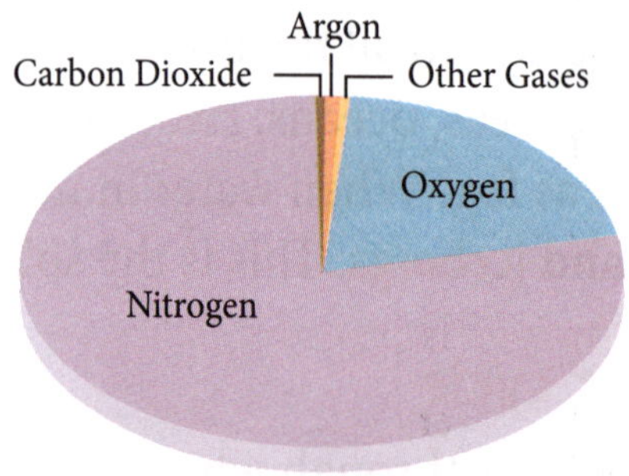

Pie Chart: Gas Composition of Atmosphere

Biosphere

The biosphere is made up of the parts of the Earth where life exists. All living things require air, water and land to survive. Thus, the biosphere includes the lithosphere, hydrosphere and atmosphere. Living things are found in land, water and air. Thus, the biosphere extends over a large area. An ecosystem is a complex community of living and non-living things functioning as a single unit. The biosphere has many ecosystems.

Green Earth

Climate change, population growth and overuse of the Earth's resources, harm the biosphere.

In a Nutshell

- The four domains of the Earth are the lithosphere, hydrosphere, atmosphere and biosphere.
- The outermost layer of the Earth is the crust, the middle layer is the mantle and the innermost layer is the core. These layers are part of the lithosphere.
- The hydrosphere consists of all the water bodies on Earth.
- The water cycle consists of processes of evaporation, condensation and precipitation.
- The blanket of air, surrounding the Earth, is the atmosphere.
- The biosphere is made up of the parts of the Earth where life exists.

Workout

A. Fill in the blanks with the correct answers.

1. The domain where human beings live is called the ....
   a. lithosphere b. stratosphere c. biosphere
2. The domain where the water cycle takes place is called the ....
   a. atmosphere b. hydrosphere c. lithosphere
3. When living and non-living things live as a unit, it is called an ....
   a. ecosystem b. water cycle c. core
4. The innermost layer of the Earth is the ....
   a. core b. crust c. mantle

B. Fill in the blanks.

1. The layer that lies below the ocean beds and continents is the ....
2. Molten rocks and minerals are found in the ....
3. .... and .... are two water bodies found in the hydrosphere.
4. The .... protects the Earth from the Sun's harmful rays.

C. Complete these sentences.

1. To survive, all living things require ....
2. The Earth's crust is made up of ....
3. Water can be found everywhere like ....
4. The three states of water are ....

D. Answer these questions in brief.

1. Name the four major domains of the Earth.
2. What is an ecosystem?
3. What does the word 'hydro' mean?
4. Name the gases found in the atmosphere.

E. Answer these questions in detail.

1. Describe the layers of the lithosphere.
2. Describe the water cycle. Draw a labelled diagram to explain it.
3. Write a short note on the biosphere.
4. What is the difference between the atmosphere and the hydrosphere?

Think Box

Why should people use sunscreen lotion or cream when they go out in the Sun?

Picture Study

Look at the picture and answer the questions.

1. Which domain of the Earth do you see in the picture?
2. What is it made up of?

Life Skills and Values

How do you think throwing waste into lakes and rivers would affect the water creatures living in there?

Enjoy

In groups of four, prepare a PowerPoint presentation on the major domains of the Earth. Each group will choose one domain. There should be at least five slides. Use pictures to explain the different components of each domain.

Weblinks

For more information, visit
https://spaceplace.nasa.gov/atmosphere/en/
https://www.natgeokids.com/au/discover/science/nature/water-cycle/
Last accessed on 31/July/2020

6 Major Landforms of the Earth

Let's learn about...

- the continents.
- different landforms—mountains, plateaus, plains, and deserts.

Key Terms

- continents
- hills
- plains
- mountains
- plateaus
- deserts
- islands
- valley
- isthmus
- sand dunes
- archipelago
- peninsula

Reflect

Identify these pictures.

....

....

....

....

The Earth, as you know, is made up of land and water. Almost two-thirds of the surface is covered with water while one-third is land. The different landforms found on the Earth are mountains, hills, plateaus, plains and deserts.

Continents

The land of the Earth is divided into seven large masses called continents. They are Asia, Australia, Africa, Europe, North America, South America and Antarctica.

Facts about continents

- Asia is the largest continent in the world.
- Australia is the world's smallest continent.

- Antarctica is a continent which is mostly covered with ice.
- Asia is the most populated continent, while Antarctica is the least populated continent.
- Australia is also known as an island continent as it is surrounded by water on all sides.

Oceans and Seas

Some continents are separated by large water bodies. The very large water bodies are called oceans. The five oceans are the Pacific Ocean, the Atlantic Ocean, the Indian Ocean, the Arctic Ocean and the Southern Ocean or the Antarctic Ocean.

The smaller water bodies are called seas. Some important seas are the Mediterranean Sea, the Black Sea, the South China Sea and the Arabian Sea.

Continents and oceans

Landforms

The Earth has an uneven surface. In some places, it is high, while in some places it is low. Let us look at some of the physical features that make up the Earth. They are known as landforms.

Mountains and hills

Mountains are the highest landforms on the Earth. The tip of the mountain is known as the peak or summit. Most mountains have steep sides or slopes with pointed peaks, but some mountains are rounded too. Some mountains are covered with snow throughout

FactPedia

The Himalayan mountain range is the highest mountain range in the world. Mount Everest in Nepal, is the highest peak in the world.

the year. A mountain range is a group or a chain of mountains that are close to each other. Mountains often have a narrow gap between them known as a mountain pass. The mountain passes help people and animals to move across the mountains.

Hills are also high landforms, but they are not as high as mountains. They are covered with grass and have a pleasant climate. So, they make great tourist spots especially in summer months. A number of hills joined together form a range of hills.

A mountain range

Hills

Figure Out
What are the names of some famous hill stations in India?

Valleys

A valley is a low area between two mountains or hills. The Kashmir valley is famous for its scenic beauty and attracts many tourists. Sometimes, a river may flow through a valley.

A valley

Plateaus

A plateau is a highland which is flat on the top. It is also called a tableland because it is raised and flat like a table. The Tibetan Plateau is the highest plateau in the world. The Deccan Plateau is located in the southern part of India.

Plateaus

Plains

Plains are large regions of flatlands. Plains are formed when hills and mountains break down due to the effect of wind and rain. They could also be formed due to the deposition of flowing lava or rock debris like silt, clay, sand or gravel brought by water, ice or wind. This happens over a very long period of time. People like to live in the plains. The soil is fertile and good for growing crops. The Great Northern Plains of India extend almost

Plains

lava: hot liquid rock that comes out of a volcano; debris: pieces of material left behind after something has been destroyed; silt: sand or mud carried by flowing water; gravel: small stones

all over North India. The Coastal Plains extend along the coasts.

An isthmus

Isthmus

An **isthmus** is a narrow strip of land that joins two large bodies of land. For example, the Isthmus of Panama that joins North and South America.

Deserts

Deserts are large areas of land that receive little or no rainfall. Only a few plants or crops grow here. They are either too hot or too cold. There are two types of deserts—hot deserts and cold deserts. Hot deserts are very hot and dry and are covered with sand. Strong winds blow the sand, leading to the formation of sand dunes. The Thar Desert in western India is an example of a hot desert. Cold deserts are covered with snow. The soil in cold deserts is always frozen making it impossible for any vegetation to grow there. Antarctica is the largest cold desert in the world.

Green Earth

The Indian Ocean has a garbage patch in the central part caused by pollution.

DIY

Look at a map of the world and find out the names of three mountains, three deserts and three oceans.

FactPedia

A volcano is a mountain with a hole on top, through which rocks, ash or lava, that are trapped inside the Earth, are thrown out.

An island

Islands

An island is a piece of land which is surrounded by water on all sides. A group or a cluster of islands, close to one another, form an archipelago. The Andaman and Nicobar Islands together form an archipelago.

A peninsula

Peninsula

A peninsula is a piece of land which has water on three sides. It is connected to a landmass on one side.

sand dunes: small sand hills

In a Nutshell

- The seven continents of the world are Asia, Europe, Africa, North America, South America, Antarctica and Australia.
- Mountains are the highest landforms on the Earth. The tip of a mountain is known as the peak.
- Hills are highlands but are not as high as mountains.
- A valley is a low area between two mountains.
- A plateau is a highland which is flat on the top. It is also known as a tableland.
- Plains are large stretches of flatland.
- Deserts are large areas of barren land with little or no rainfall.
- An island is a piece of land which is surrounded by water on all sides.

Workout

A. Fill in the blanks.

1. The most populated continent in the world is ...., while the least populated one is ....
2. A .... is a piece of land which has water on three sides.
3. People go across the mountains through the ....
4. The .... Desert is in the western part of India.

B. Name the following.

1. A tableland ....
2. A lowland between two mountains ....
3. An island continent ....
4. The largest cold desert ....

C. Answer these questions in brief.

1. What is a mountain range?
2. Why is a plateau called a tableland?
3. Why are the plains densely populated?
4. Why do people like to visit hill stations during summer?

D. Answer these questions in detail.

1. How are plains formed?
2. What are the two types of deserts? How are they similar to and different from one another?
3. What is an isthmus?

E. Map Work

Using an atlas, mark the following on an outline of the world map.

- The Himalayas in Asia
- The Alps in Europe
- The Gobi Desert in Asia
- The Rocky Mountains in North America
- The Sahara Desert in Africa

Think Box

It is said that life on a mountain is difficult. Do you agree or disagree? Give reasons for your answer.

Picture Study

Look at the picture and answer the questions.

1. What kind of landform is this?
2. Why can't you see any plants here?
3. How is the climate here?

Life Skills and Values

Tour Brochure:

You are a travel guide working in a group with your friends. Each group chooses a landform. Now, plan a travel brochure giving the details of the landform, inviting tourists to come and visit it. Paste pictures and provide other details such as travelling dates, climate information and places of interest. Add two precautions for the tourist.

Enjoy

Play a game

Draw a table with four columns named mountains, hills, plains and deserts. Now, choose a letter and use an atlas to find the names of landforms that start with that letter. The one with the maximum number of names wins the game.

Weblinks

For more information, visit
https://www.nationalgeographic.org/encyclopedia/Continent/4th-grade/
https://kids.nationalgeographic.com/explore/nature/habitats/mountain/
Last accessed on 31/July/2020

7 Water Bodies

Let's learn about...

- oceans of the world.
- water bodies—oceans, seas, lakes and rivers.
- some other water bodies.

Key Terms

- oceans
- bays
- seas
- rivers
- straits
- lakes
- snow-fed river
- rain-fed river

Reflect

Where can you find these?

....

We have learnt that water covers most of the Earth's surface. The Earth is the only planet where water can be found in its liquid state. Let us now learn about the large and small water bodies of the Earth.

Ocean

An ocean is a large and deep area of water. The water in an ocean is salty. You already know that the five oceans in the world are the Pacific Ocean, the Indian Ocean, the Atlantic Ocean, the Arctic Ocean and the Southern Ocean.

Facts about oceans

- The Pacific Ocean is the largest ocean in the world. The Atlantic Ocean is the second largest.

- The Mariana Trench in the Pacific Ocean is the deepest point on the Earth's surface.
- All the oceans are connected to one other in some way or the other.
- The Arctic Ocean is almost covered in ice during winter.
- Waves are formed due to the effect of wind on water.
- Earthquakes under the water leads to formation of huge tidal waves called **tsunami**, that can cause a lot of damage.
- Oceans are home to many marine creatures such as whales, dolphins, sharks, octopuses and crabs.

> **Figure Out**
> Why is the water in oceans and seas salty?

> **Green Earth**
> Glaciers of the world are melting much faster than they did in the past. This is due to global warming which is caused by pollution.

Sea

A **sea** is a large area of water but it is not as big as an ocean. Sea water is also salty. The Arabian Sea borders India on the west.

River

A **river** is a body of freshwater flowing across the land. The source of a river is mostly from a mountain or a hill. It flows down as a stream and finally becomes broader as it enters the plains. Most rivers end in larger water bodies, such as oceans, seas or lakes.

The Ganga

There are two types of rivers—**snow-fed rivers** and **rain-fed rivers**. Snow-fed rivers are formed due to the melting of snow or glaciers. The Ganga is a snow-fed river. Rain-fed rivers are formed due to rainfall. Tapi and Narmada are rain-fed rivers.

A shikara on the Dal Lake

Lake

A **lake** is a body of water surrounded by land on all sides. Dal, Wular, Loktak and Chilka are a few examples.

> **FactPedia**
> The Caspian Sea located between Europe and Asia is the largest lake in the world. It is called a sea because of its large size.

Bay

A bay is a large body of water connected to an ocean or sea formed by an inlet of land. It normally has a wide mouth. The Bay of Bengal is an example.

Strait

A strait is a narrow channel of sea joining two larger expanses of water. The Palk Strait is located between Tamil Nadu in India and the northern part of Sri Lanka. It connects the Bay of Bengal in the northeast with Palk Bay in the southwest.

The Pamban bridge on Palk Strait

DIY

If you were to live in the desert region for seven days where there is water scarcity, how would you adapt to the lifestyle? Think and write about it, keeping in mind water scarcity in the region.

In a Nutshell

- An ocean is a very large area of water.
- There are five oceans in the world. They are the Pacific Ocean, the Indian Ocean, the Atlantic Ocean, the Arctic Ocean and the Southern Ocean.
- A river is a fresh water body flowing across the land. It usually flows into the sea.
- A lake is a body of water surrounded by land on all sides.
- A bay and a strait are other kinds of water bodies on the Earth.

Workout

A. Fill in the blanks.

1. The water in the oceans and seas is ....
2. An earthquake under the sea causes tidal waves called ....
3. The .... is located between Tamil Nadu in India and the northern part of Sri Lanka.
4. A .... is a body of freshwater flowing across the land.

inlet: a narrow strip of water that stretches into the land from the sea or a lake or between islands

B. Who am I?

1. I am the largest ocean: ....
2. I am a body of water surrounded by land on all sides: ....
3. I am a snow-fed river: ....
4. I am the largest lake in the world: ....

C. Answer these questions in brief.

1. Name the five oceans in the world.
2. What are rain-fed rivers?
3. Why can't we drink water from the oceans and seas?

D. Answer these questions.

1. What are the different types of rivers? Explain, using examples.
2. How is a strait different from an isthmus?
3. Give one difference and one similarity between oceans and seas.

E. **Map Work**

1. Using an atlas, mark these landforms in every continent and write their names, on an outline map of the world.

- River
- Bay
- Strait
- Sea
- Lake
- Five oceans

Think Box

Why is the land on both sides of a river very fertile?

Picture Study

Look at the picture and answer the questions.

1. Identify this place under the ocean.
2. Where do you think it is located?
3. Why is this place significant?

Life Skills and Values

Wells and tube wells are important sources of water, especially in rural India. What will happen if the underground water table reduces severely?

Enjoy

You know that the water from the seas and oceans evaporates on being heated and comes down in the form of rain. Yet, rainwater is not salty. Let us find out why rainwater is not salty with the help of an experiment.

1. Dissolve some salt in a glass of water.
2. Keep adding salt until it no longer dissolves in water. Note down the number of teaspoons you have added.
3. Leave the glass of water in a warm place for a few hours. You will notice that the water will evaporate and leave the salt behind.

The heat of the sun evaporates the water from seas, rivers and lakes, leaving the salt behind. When this water condenses to form rain, it is salt free and that is why rainwater is not salty.

Weblinks

For more information, visit
https://kids.nationalgeographic.com/explore/nature/habitats/ocean/
https://www.nationalgeographic.org/encyclopedia/river/
Last accessed on 31/July/2020

Across the Boundary 2

Crossword

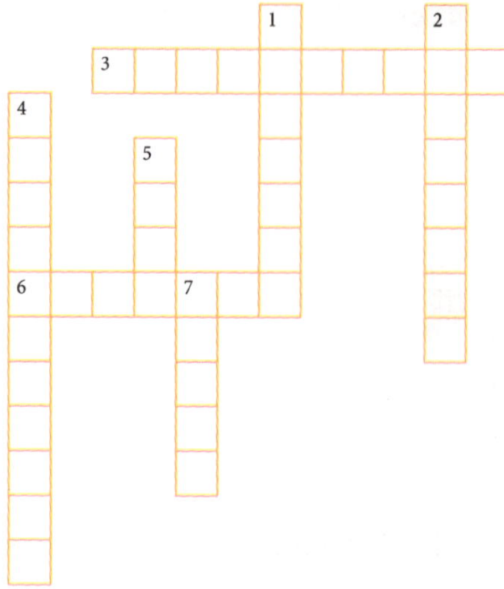

Across

3. Movement of the Earth around the Sun
6. They are caused by the revolution of the Earth

Down

1. The heavenly bodies that move around the sun
2. Spinning of the Earth on its axis
4. The two halves of the Earth formed by the equator
5. The imaginary vertical line on which the Earth moves
7. The path taken by the planets to move around the Sun

Research

Draw the different layers of the atmosphere. Use the internet to find out the layers in which you will find the following:

- Weather
- Aircraft
- Satellites
- Ozone layer
- Shooting stars

Map Skills

Write the names of two countries that lie in the northern and southern hemispheres each.

Word Search

Find the names of the following seas in the given word grid.

Coral	Red
Mediterranean	Dead
Black	North
Norwegian	Carribean
Arabian	Caspian
Adriatic	Aegean

K	N	R	C	S	B	C	A	H	Q	B	W
N	A	V	U	I	C	B	L	A	C	K	R
Z	E	O	N	N	A	R	T	T	R	M	X
D	N	A	A	O	R	Y	D	W	Y	T	Z
X	A	E	R	C	R	I	B	I	D	A	S
S	R	G	A	O	I	W	D	M	P	H	F
A	R	E	B	R	B	M	E	P	G	M	H
D	E	A	I	A	E	W	R	G	Q	O	D
R	T	N	A	L	A	R	P	K	I	R	R
I	I	Q	N	X	N	Z	W	R	U	A	W
A	D	N	O	R	T	H	L	G	Z	C	N
T	E	N	L	C	A	S	P	I	A	N	C
I	M	E	J	D	A	E	D	M	W	T	R
C	P	X	Q	Q	V	E	L	B	H	M	M

8 Types of Maps

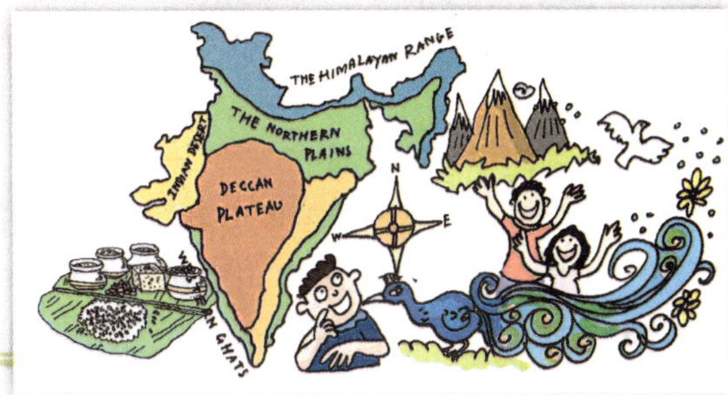

Let's learn about...

- types of maps.
- scale of a map.
- symbols used on a map.
- use of colours on a map.

Key Terms

- thematic map
- physical map
- political map
- atlas
- cartographer
- legend or key
- scale
- symbols

Reflect

Look at the map of the zoo and answer these questions

The City Zoo

1. To see the giraffe, in which direction should you move from the entrance? ....
2. You want to see the crocodile after seeing the giraffe. In which direction should you move?.........................
3. After a snack at the restaurant, if you want to see the lion and the tiger, in which direction should you move?.........................
4. If you are facing the camel's enclosure, in which direction are the enclosures of the horse, the elephant, and the bird?.........................

Maps

Maps are drawings of the Earth on a flat surface. It shows the whole or a part of an area. Unlike a globe, a map can give us detailed information about a place, such as landforms, cities, towns, altitude, physical features, continents and roads. A map can be carried easily. An atlas is a book of maps. A person who prepares a map is called a cartographer.

Types of Maps

The two main types of maps are physical and political maps. A physical map shows the physical features of a continent, country or some landforms, such as mountains, hills, rivers and lakes. We use different colours and symbols to show the physical features on a map. A political map shows the national boundary, states of a country, location of cities and capital cities.

FactPedia

The top of a map always shows the north direction.

Political map of India

Physical map of India

Apart from physical and political maps, there are other types of maps, such as road maps, climatic maps, tourist maps, maps showing rainfall, natural vegetation or crops, industries and population. These maps are called thematic maps. Some thematic maps also show routes in a forest, zoo or an amusement park.

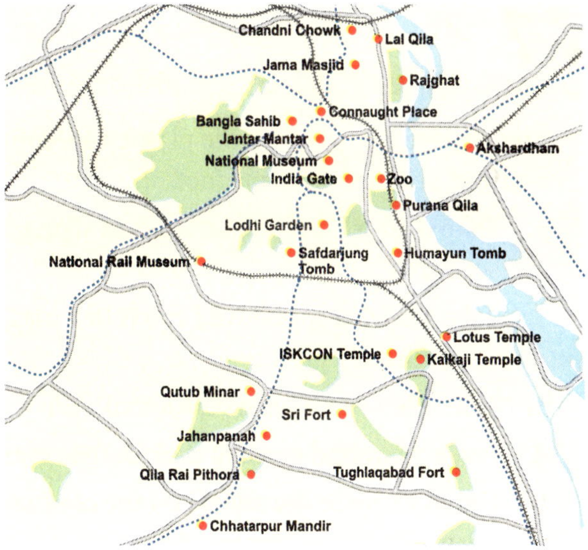

Thematic map

Scale

A map represents a large area of land. For convenience, a map is reduced in size to fit a page or a screen. To measure distance on a map, we use a map scale. The scale of a map shows the relationship between the distances on a map and the actual distances between two places on the ground. For example, if the scale used is 1 cm for 100 km, then 2 cm shows an actual distance of 200 km. Different maps use different scales. For example, while showing a road map of a city, we may use the scale of 1 cm = 1 km on the actual ground. For a world map, we may use the scale of 1 cm = 1000 km on the ground. All maps are drawn to a scale which is shown on the map.

FactPedia

A road map helps a tourist not only to find the exact location of a place, but also to plan an interesting trip.

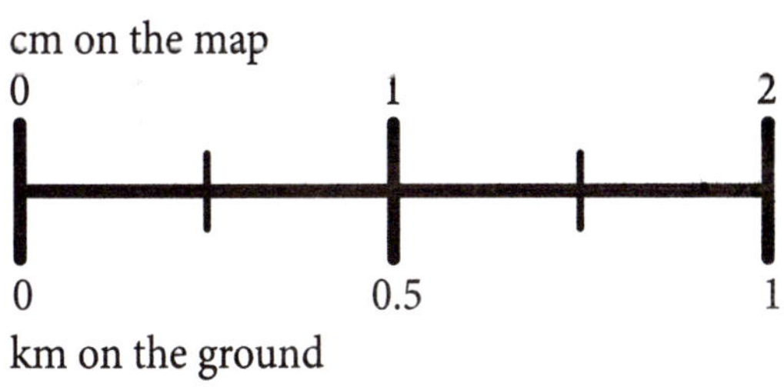

Scale

Green Earth

Many cities adopt different measures to reduce pollution. Find out if there are such measures in the city where you live.

Compass

An easy way to find directions is with the help of a compass. It has a needle that always points to the north. If we know one direction, it is easy to find the others.

A compass

DIY

Make a simple compass

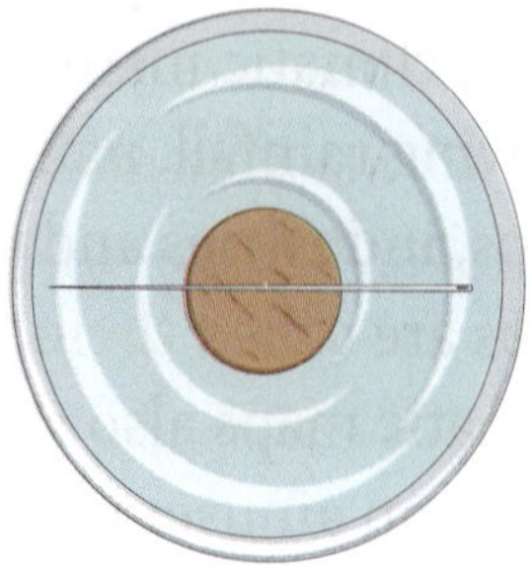

You require a bowl or a wide plastic cap, some water, a cork, a needle, a pair of scissors and a magnet.

1. Take the cork and ask an adult to slice a round piece using the scissors.
2. Take a sewing needle and rub it to a magnet twenty times in the same direction.
3. Take a bowl or a wide plastic cap. Add some water to it.
4. Place the round piece of cork in the centre of the bowl of water.
5. Carefully place the needle on the cork and watch. The needle will slowly turn towards the north. Your compass is ready!

Symbols

To make a map easier to read, we use **symbols**. Symbols are simple drawings used to represent different things. A **legend** or a **key** is given on the map to explain what the symbols stand for. Different types of lines and icons are used to show the different features, such as roads, railway tracks and highways. The symbols make it easier for us to locate these features on a map.

Bus station	Museum
Taxi stand	School
Metro station	Food court
Train station	Public toilet
Airport	Telephone
Sea port	Petrol station
Factory	Resting area

Signs and symbols

Colours

When we look at a map, we see that it has different colours. These colours represent different physical features. Varying shades of these colours on a map show different heights and depths. For example, different shades of blue show the varied depths of seas and oceans. The darker the blue, the greater is the depth, while the lighter the blue, the lesser is the depth. The dark green colour indicates lowlands, while light green indicates hills and plateaus. A mountain is represented in brown. The darker the shade of brown, the higher is the mountain. Purple is used to show the highest mountains. Usually, the key explains what each colour stands for.

Figure Out

What is the full form of GPS and how does it work? How does it help us travel from one place to another?

In a Nutshell

- Maps are drawings of the Earth on a flat surface.
- Maps are mostly of two types—physical and political.
- Apart from physical and political maps, there are thematic maps too.
- To measure distance on a map, we use a map scale.
- Symbols are used to represent different features on a map.
- We use different colours to show different physical features, their height or depth on a map.

Workout

A. Fill in the blanks.

1. A map is a .... of the Earth on a flat surface.
2. All maps are drawn to a ....
3. The brown colour on a map represents ....
4. The different colours on a physical map show different ....

B. Who am I?

1. I am a book of maps: ....
2. I draw maps: ....
3. I explain the symbols used on a map: ....
4. I show the physical features of a country: ....

C. Answer these questions in brief.

1. What are thematic maps?
2. What is a compass?
3. The scale of a map is 1 cm = 100 km. What is the distance between two places if the distance between them is 5 cm on the map?
4. Why is it important to have a legend or a key on a map?

D. Answer these questions.

1. Why is a map more useful than a globe?
2. How is a physical map different from a political map?
3. Why do we use different colours on a map?
4. Why do we use symbols on a map?

Think Box

What problems do you think you would have to face if a cartographer forgets to use colours on a physical map?

Picture Study

Look at the map and answer these questions.

1. What kind of a map is this?
2. What does it tell us?

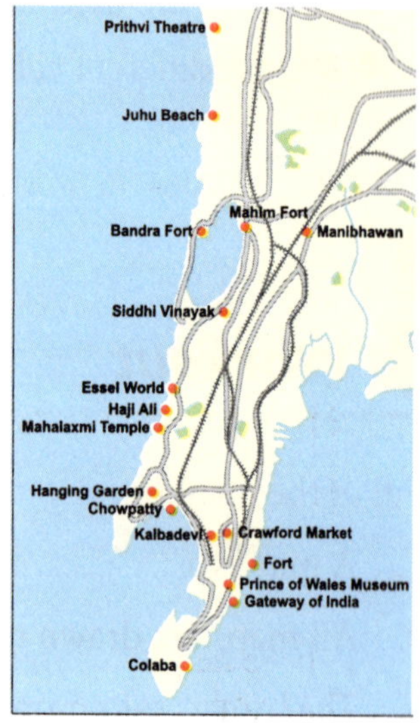

Life Skills and Values

Which one do you think is more useful while travelling—maps or globes?

Enjoy

A. In groups of four, draw a map for a new city. Use symbols and colours to show all the interesting features the city will have. Make a legend or a key to explain what the colours and symbols represent. Present the map in the classroom.

B. Make your own symbols for these geographical features.

- Forest
- School
- Park
- Hotel
- Police station
- Railway station
- Hospital
- Restaurant

Weblinks

For more information, visit
http://www.planetware.com/cartography-and-maps-for-beginners.htm
https://www.nationalgeographic.org/encyclopedia/map/5th-grade/
Last accessed on 31/July/2020

9 States of India

Let's learn about...

- the states of India.
- the water boundaries.
- the neighbouring countries.

Key Terms

- state
- district
- neighbouring countries
- state capital
- governor
- union territory
- chief minister
- secretariat

Reflect

Look at the map of few countries in Europe and answer these questions.

1. Name three neighbouring countries of France.
2. Name the capital of France.
3. Name two water bodies near France.

States of India

India is a very vast country. For administrative purposes, the country is divided into smaller divisions called states. India has 28 states and 8 union territories. Each state and union territory has a capital. New Delhi is the national capital of India. Each state is further divided into districts and subdistricts called tehsils, taluks, blocks or *mandals*.

FactPedia

Each state has a governor who lives in an official residence called Raj Bhavan.

A chief minister is the administrative head of a state. The state capital is where the chief ministers have their office, ministries and secretariat.

The political map given shows all the states and union territories of India.

Political map of India

India is a peninsula surrounded by water on three sides and by land on one side. The Arabian Sea lies on the west of the Indian peninsula, the Bay of Bengal lies to its east and the Indian Ocean is in the south. The neighbouring countries of India are Nepal, Bhutan, Pakistan, Bangladesh, Afghanistan, Sri Lanka, Maldives, China and Myanmar.

Look at the map of India and name one neighbouring country that surrounds India in these directions:

North: .... South: ....

North-west: .... North-east: ....

States	Capital City	States	Capital City
Andhra Pradesh	Amaravati	Manipur	Imphal
Arunachal Pradesh	Itanagar	Meghalaya	Shillong
Assam	Dispur	Mizoram	Aizawl
Bihar	Patna	Nagaland	Kohima
Chhattisgarh	Raipur	Odisha (Orissa)	Bhubaneshwar
Goa	Panaji	Punjab	Chandigarh (shared with Haryana)
Gujarat	Gandhinagar	Rajasthan	Jaipur
Haryana	Chandigarh (shared with Punjab)	Sikkim	Gangtok
Himachal Pradesh	Shimla	Tamil Nadu	Chennai
Jharkhand	Ranchi	Telangana	Hyderabad
Karnataka	Bengaluru	Tripura	Agartala
Kerala	Thiruvananthapuram	Uttar Pradesh	Lucknow
Madhya Pradesh	Bhopal	Uttarakhand	Dehradun
Maharashtra	Mumbai	West Bengal	Kolkata

Union Territories	Capital City	Union Territories	Capital City
Andaman and Nicobar Islands	Port Blair	Jammu and Kashmir	Srinagar (Summer); Jammu (Winter)
Chandigarh	Chandigarh	Ladakh	Leh
Dadra and Nagar Haveli and Daman and Diu	Daman	Lakshadweep	Kavaratti
Delhi – National Capital Territory	Delhi	Puducherry (Pondicherry)	Pondicherry

Green Earth

New Delhi, India's capital city, is one of the most polluted cities in the world. Why do you think this is so?

FactPedia

A union territory has its own elected government ruled directly by the Central Government.

DIY

Answer these questions about the state in which you live.

Name of your state ....

Name of its capital ....

Name two neighbouring states ....

Name the town/city you live in ....

Name the landforms in your state ....

Name the river flowing through the state, if any ....

General climate of your state ....

Famous crop grown in your state ....

In a Nutshell

- India has 28 states and 8 union territories.
- Each state and union territory has a capital.
- New Delhi is the national capital of India.
- India is a peninsula surrounded by water on three sides and by land on one side.
- The neighbouring countries of India are Nepal, Bhutan, Pakistan, Bangladesh, Afghanistan, Sri Lanka, Maldives, China and Myanmar.

Figure Out

Which state was India's capital state before New Delhi?

Workout

A. Fill in the blanks.

1. India is a .... country.
2. A .... map shows the administrative divisions.
3. The .... is the administrative head of the state.
4. The .... Sea is on the west of India.

B. Match the columns.

	Column A		Column B
1.	Madhya Pradesh	a.	Raipur
2.	Chhattisgarh	b.	Chennai
3.	Uttar Pradesh	c.	Mumbai
4.	Andaman and Nicobar	d.	Bhopal
5.	Maharashtra	e.	Panaji
6.	Tamil Nadu	f.	Dehradun
7.	Uttarakhand	g.	Lucknow
8.	Goa	h.	Port Blair

C. Fill in the blanks with the correct answers.

1. The states are divided into smaller ....
   a. districts b. nations c. secretariats
2. The capital of Dadra and Nagar Haveli and Daman and Diu is ....
   a. Dadra b. Kavaratti c. Daman
3. Landmass surrounded by water on three sides and land on one side is called a ....
   a. plateau b. plain c. peninsula
4. The .... forms the eastern boundary of India.
   a. Arabian Sea b. Bay of Bengal c. Indian Ocean

D. Answer these questions orally.

1. Who is the administrative head of a state?
2. Name the three water boundaries of India.
3. Which country lies to the west of India?

E. Answer these questions.

1. Name the countries that share a border with India.
2. Why is India divided into states?
3. Name the political divisions of India.

F. Map Work

On an outline map of India, mark and colour all the states and union territories.

Think Box

Why do you think New Delhi is the national capital of India?

Picture Study

Look at the picture and answer the questions.

1. Which continent does this map represent?
2. Name India's neighbouring countries.
3. Which country is the biggest in the continent?

Life Skills and Values

A group of travellers have to visit your state from a neighbouring country. How would you help them to travel within the state as they do not understand the local language?

Enjoy

Work in groups in the class. On an outline political map of India, mark the state capitals. Each group can take five states. Find out the names of the chief ministers of these states. Collect more information about the chosen states and make a powerpoint presentation to share with the class.

Weblinks

For more information, visit
https://knowindia.gov.in/states-uts/
https://www.incredibleindia.org/content/incredibleindia/en/destinations/states.html
Last accessed on 31/July/2020

10 India–Physical Divisions

Let's learn about...

- the physical or geographical regions of India.
- the climate of India.
- the vegetation of India.
- the crops grown in India.

Key Terms

- The Northern Mountains
- The Northern Plains
- The Desert Region
- The Peninsular Plateau
- The Coastal regions
- The Islands
- Himalayas
- Indo-Gangetic Plains

Reflect

Look at this map of the world. You can see India marked with a circle. Discuss the shape of the country. What do you see on the three sides of our country? What do you see on the northern side of India?

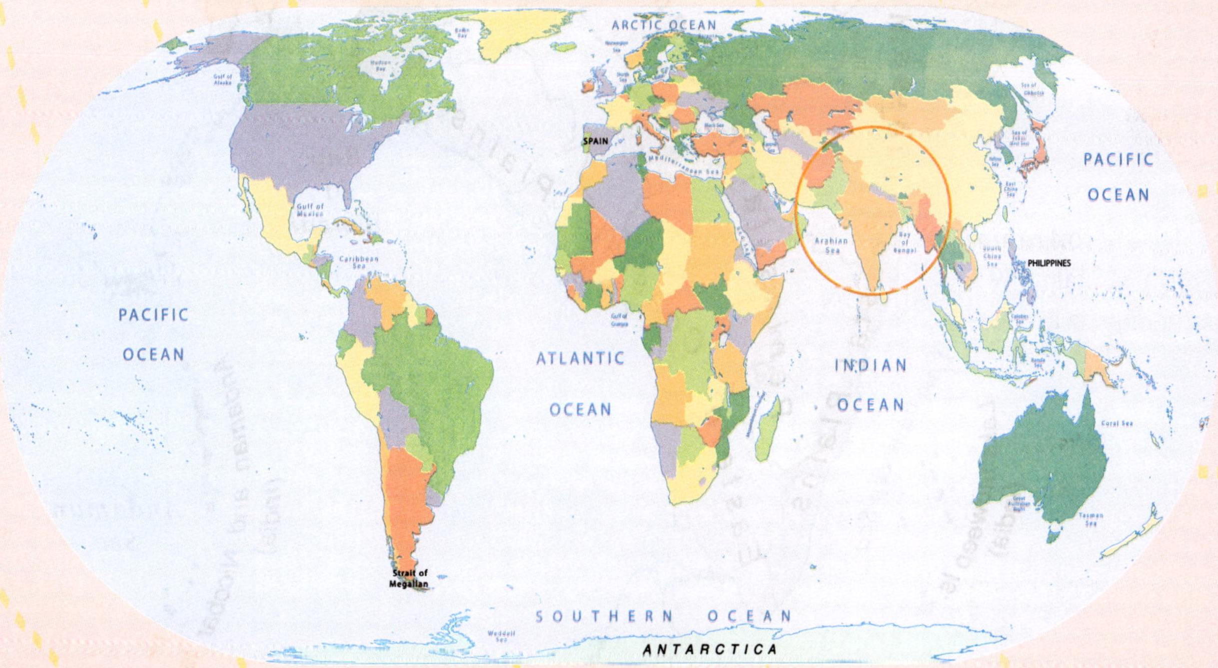

Physical Divisions in India

The physical divisions of a country indicate the way regions are divided on the basis of landforms and its geography.

Look the map given here. You will see that India is divided into six geographical regions:

- The Northern Mountains
- The Northern Plains
- The Desert Region
- The Peninsular Plateau
- The Coastal Regions
- The Islands

India: Physical

Northern Mountains

Northern Mountains

In the northern part of India lies a huge mountain range called the Himalayas. It extends from Jammu and Kashmir in the north to Arunachal Pradesh in the east. The Himalayas have some of the highest mountain peaks in the world which are covered with snow throughout the year. The highest mountain peak is Mount Everest in Nepal. Some of the states and union territories of India that are located in this region are Jammu and Kashmir, Ladakh, Himachal Pradesh, Uttarakhand, Sikkim, Arunachal Pradesh and the northern part of West Bengal.

The Himalayas can be divided into three ranges:

- Himadri (greater Himalayas)
- Himachal (middle Himalayas)
- Shiwalik (lesser Himalayas)

Himadri: The Himadri range is covered in snow and has extreme cold weather. There are glaciers in the region which are the source of many rivers. No vegetation can be seen in these regions.

Himachal: The regions in Himachal range have cool summers and cold winters. There are many hill stations such as Shimla, Nainital, Shillong, Darjiling, Manali and many more in this region. Tourists go to these places in winters to see the snowfall. Trees such as pine, deodar, oak grow in the region. People grow a variety of fruits such as apples and peaches in orchards and cultivate tea in the plantations.

FactPedia
Some of the hills in the north-east are the Mizo Hills, the Khasi Hills, and the Garo Hills.

Shiwalik: In the Shiwalik range, the weather becomes warm in summers and remains cool in winters. Farmers practise terrace- farming and grow potatoes, rice and wheat. This range is good for cultivating medicinal plants.

Importance of the Himalayas

- The Himalayas act as a barrier to protect our country from the cold winds from Central Asia, so that the Northern Plains remain warm.

Kanchenjunga at sunrise

barrier: an object like a fence that prevents people from moving forward from one place to another

- The Himalayas stop the rainbearing monsoon winds from going further north. As a result, the northern plains, receive a good amount of rainfall.
- The Himalayas are the source of perennial rivers flowing in the north Indian states which makes the plains fertile.
- The forests on the Himalayan slopes provide home to many animals and are a source of forest products like timber and medicines.

Northern Plains

The Northern Plains of India extend from the south of the Himalayas to the north of the Deccan Plateau. The region is drained by many important rivers that originate in the Himalayas. The Ganga, which is the largest river in India, along with its tributaries flows through the Northern Plains. The other rivers are the Brahmaputra and the Indus, and their tributaries.

The Northern Plains

The Northern Plains are made of fertile alluvial soil deposited by these rivers. This soil is ideal for the cultivation of wheat and rice. Therefore, the Northern Plains are also known as the 'food bowl of India.' The plains are usually hot in the summer and cold in the winter.

Trees such as peepal, banyan, neem, sheesham and eucalyptus grow here. Crops like wheat and rice are grown here. The Northern Plains are thickly populated. Punjab, Haryana, Assam, Uttar Pradesh, West Bengal and the union territory of Delhi are situated in this region.

Importance of the Northern Plains

The Northern plains are important as:

- they provide fertile alluvial soil for agriculture, to grow food crops for the nation.
- they receive adequate rainfall to make perennial rivers.
- the rivers are navigable and used as inland waterways.
- the flat area is good for settlements, agriculture and trade.
- the area has thickly populated cities.
- they have a good network of rail and road which helps the industries to grow.

FactPedia

Major river basins in the Northern Plains are formed by the river Indus in the east, river Ganga in the centre and river Brahmaputra in the east.

tributary: a stream or river that flows into a larger one; fertile: land or soil that plants grow well in; alluvial: soil made of sand and earth that is left by rivers or floods; perennial: rivers that have water throughout the year; navigable: easy to move around in

The Desert

The Thar Desert

The northwestern part of India is dry and sandy. This region gets little or no rainfall. Hence, hardly anything grows in this area. This region is called the Thar Desert or the Great Indian Desert. It is very hot and dry in the summers and very cold in the winters. There are not many people living in the desert region. The desert region includes most of Rajasthan and some parts of Gujarat. The natural vegetation includes cactus and acacia. Cotton, oil seeds and millets are grown here. When the wind blows, it carries sand from one area to another, forming mounds of sand. These are known as sand dunes.

The Peninsular Plateau

Figure Out
What do we call a dust storm in a desert?

The Peninsular Plateau has three parts—the Malwa Plateau, the Chota Nagpur Plateau and the Deccan Plateau. The Peninsular Plateau located towards south of India is separated from the Northern Plains by the Vindhaya and Satpura range of hills. Malwa Plateau lies towards the west and the Chota Nagpur Plateau is in the north east of the Peninsular Plateau. Deccan Plateau is a triangle shaped plateau, located south of the Peninsular plateau covering many areas in the region.

The Peninsular Plateau

It borders the Chota Nagpur Plateau and Satpura Range on one side and mountains, known as the Eastern and Western Ghats, on the other sides of the triangle.

Many rivers flow through the Peninsular Plateau. The Krishna, the Kaveri, the Mahanadi and the Godavari rivers flow from the west to the east as the plateau slopes eastwards. The Narmada and the Tapi rivers flow from the east to the west merging with the Arabian Sea. The climate of the region is very hot in the summer and cold in the winter. Madhya Pradesh, Chhattisgarh, Jharkhand, Telangana and parts of Tamil Nadu, Karnataka, Maharashtra, Andhra Pradesh, Odisha are located in this region.

The Deccan Plateau region is rich in black soil which is suitable for growing cotton. A variety of trees grow here depending on the amount of rainfall the region receives. Thorny scrub forest and broad-leafed trees are found in some regions.

FactPedia
The Nilgiri Hills or the blue mountains are located in the southern part of the Deccan Plateau.

acacia: the babool tree

Importance of the Peninsular Plateau

- Peninsular Plateau region is known as the storehouse of minerals in India. These minerals provide raw material for various manufacturing industries.
- The black soil in the Deccan Plateau region makes it the largest cotton growing region of India.
- The largest coal producing belt in India lies in the plateau region.
- The dams, built on the rivers flowing through the uneven hard plateau, make the Peninsular Plateau a major area for producing hydroelectricity.

The Coastal Region

Coastal Region

The Eastern Coastal Plain lies between the Bay of Bengal and the Eastern Ghats. It is neither too hot, nor too cold here. The four major rivers—the Mahanadi, the Godavari, the Krishna and the Kaveri—flow through this region into the Bay of Bengal. The climate is hot and humid in summer and winter is mild. The southern part of this region receives rain during winter. The hilly regions are cooler than the plains.

The Western Coastal Plain lies between the Arabian Sea and the Western Ghats. The Narmada and the Tapi rivers flow through this region. Tamil Nadu, Andhra Pradesh and Odisha lie on the eastern side along the Eastern Coastal Plain. Kerala, Karnataka, Goa and Maharashtra lie on the western side of the Western Coastal Plains.

The Islands

Andaman Islands

There are two groups of islands in India—the Andaman and Nicobar Islands in the Bay of Bengal and the Lakshadweep Islands in the Arabian Sea. The main crop grown here is rice. Coconut trees and many evergreen trees, with woody climbers, are found here. Orchids and a variety of ferns also thrive here. The Islands have a hot and humid weather with mild winters. These regions are very scenic and attract many tourists.

evergreen trees: trees that do not shed their leaves and stay green throughout the year

Green Earth

Increasing construction activities in the Lakshadweep islands lead to pollution and affect the climate, the corals and the beaches.

DIY

Find out the names of the other sea creatures and plants that live on and around coral reefs.

Coral reefs are actually tiny little animals called polyps. Polyps live on the outside of the reef. As polyps die, they become hard and new polyps grow on top of them, causing the reef to grow. The Lakshadweep Islands are home to some of the largest coral reefs in the Indian Ocean.

In a Nutshell

- India is divided into six geographical regions—the Northern Mountains, the Northern Plains, the Desert Region, the Peninsular Plateau, the Coastal Region and the Islands.
- The Northern Mountains can be divided into the Himadri, Himachal and Shiwalik ranges.
- The Northern Plains are very fertile and many rivers flow through it.
- The Thar Desert or the Great Indian Desert lies in the north-western part of India.
- The Peninsular Plateau region is divided into the Malwa, Chota Nagpur and Deccan Plateau.
- The Andaman and Nicobar Islands in the Bay of Bengal and Lakshadweep Islands in the Arabian Sea are two island regions of India.

Workout

A. Write T for true and F for false.

1. The Himalayas are the highest mountain range in the world. ☐
2. The Andaman and Nicobar Islands are in the Arabian Sea. ☐
3. The Deccan Plateau region is rich in black soil. ☐
4. The river Yamuna flows through the Northern Plains. ☐
5. The Thar Desert is densely populated. ☐

B. Name the following.

1. The Himalayan range where medicinal plants are cultivated: ....
2. The Great Indian Desert: ....

3. Islands in the Arabian Sea: ....

4. Two rivers that flow through the Northern Plains ....

C. Answer these questions in brief.

1. What is a peninsula?
2. Name the states located in the northern mountains region.
3. What are sand dunes?
4. Name two rivers that flow through the Deccan Plateau into the Arabian Sea.

D. Answer these questions in detail.

1. Explain the difference between the climate of the Northern Mountains and the Northern Plains.
2. What is the importance of the Himalayas for our country?
3. Why is the Peninsular Plateau region important for India?
4. Write a short note on the Islands of India.

E. Map Work

On an outline map of India, mark the following regions.

1. The Northern Mountains
2. The Northern Plains
3. The Thar Desert
4. The Coastal Plains
5. The Peninsular Plateau
6. The Islands
7. The Arabian Sea, Bay of Bengal and the Indian Ocean

Think Box

Long ago, many foreigners and sometimes enemies came to India by crossing the Himalayas. Why do you think they followed that route?

Picture Study

Look at the picture and answer these questions.

1. Which region is shown in the picture?
2. What do you think is not easily available here?
3. What kind of plants grow here?

Life Skills and Values

The hill stations in India are slowly becoming warmer and polluted due to influx of tourists. If you were travelling in a hilly area in India, which two precautions would you take to prevent pollution?

Enjoy

A. List names of five fruits and name the states where they are grown. Mark all those states on a political map of India.

B. Team up with another classmate from your class and find out about one state. Have a class discussion. You will learn a lot about India.

Weblinks

For more information, visit
https://www.visibleearth.nasa.gov/images/69229/great-indian-desert?size=all
https://knowindia.gov.in/profile/geological-structure.php
Last accessed on 31/July/2020

11 Major Rivers of India

Let's learn about...

- the major rivers flowing through India.
- perennial and non-perennial rivers.

Key Terms

- perennial
- non-perennial
- seasonal
- river basin
- delta
- estuary

Reflect

Unscramble the names of some rivers given below.

AKIHNRS	....	IPTA	....	VKERAI	....
NAGGA	....	IMDAHANA	....	MDAAARN	....

India is a land with many rivers—some rise in the Northern Himalayas, others have their source in the ranges in central or southern India. Most of these rivers have dams built across them.

Journey of a River

The journey of a river starts from its source in the mountain and it flows down rapidly towards the plains. It may branch out into tributaries while flowing towards the sea or the ocean. Towards the end of its journey, a river merges with the sea or the ocean.

DIY

Look at how a river travels from its source to the mouth. Write a paragraph describing its journey.

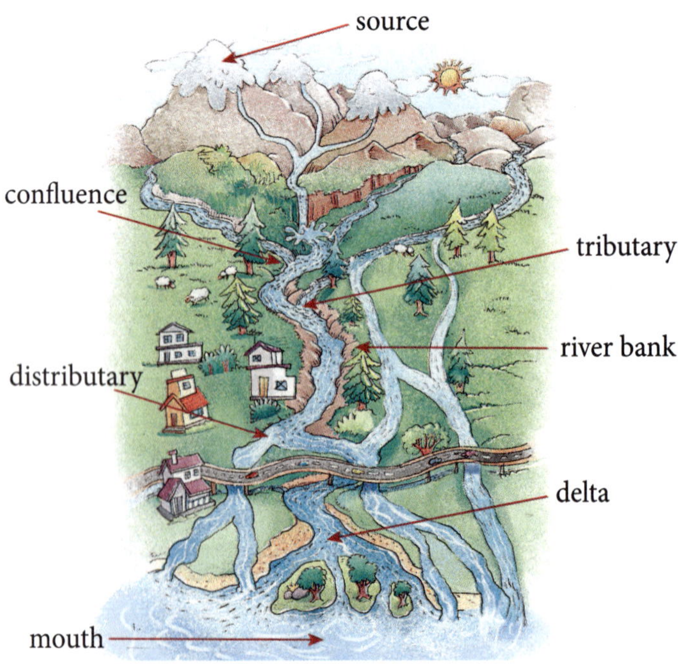

Major Rivers in India

There are two kinds of rivers that flow through the land. The first kind has water throughout the year, like the Ganga, the Yamuna and the Kaveri. These are called perennial rivers. The rivers that get water only during the monsoons, that is, the rainy season are called non-perennial or seasonal rivers. The seasonal rivers are rain-fed and have very little water during the summer and winter months, like the Tapi and the Narmada. Each river has a river basin. It is an area of land around the river with streams running down into it.

> **Green Earth**
> Rivers are the lifeline of the regions to which they belong. We must keep them clean.

Perennial rivers

There are many rivers that flow through the Indo-Gangetic Plain forming a network of rivers. The Ganga rises in the Gangotri Glacier in the state of Uttarakhand and is known as Bhagirathi river. At Devprayag, the confluence of Bhagirathi takes place with the river Alaknanda and this large river is then called, the Ganga. The Yamuna rises in the Yamunotri Glacier in the Himalayas. Both rivers flow eastwards through several states.

> **FactPedia**
> The Ganga Delta at Sunderbans in West Bengal is the largest delta in the world.

The Ganga, Yamuna and another river called the Saraswati, meet at Allahabad at a place called Triveni Sangam. The Gomti, Ghaghara, Gandak and Son rivers join the Ganga on its journey. The Betwa, and Chambal rivers join the Yamuna river.

The mighty Ganga, also called the Ganges, flows eastwards, entering Bengal. The Hooghly river is a distributary of the Ganga as it enters the Bay of Bengal. Some rivers, before entering a sea, branch out into smaller rivers, forming a delta.

Confluence of Alaknanda and Bhagirathi rivers at Devprayag

Rivers Chenab and Jhelum flow through Jammu and Kashmir. Sutlej, Ravi and Beas are the major rivers that flow through Punjab and Himachal Pradesh. As we move down to Central India, we see two rivers, Tapi and Narmada, that rise in the Satpura and the Vindhya ranges. These rivers flow into the Arabian Sea in one stream called an estuary. They do not slow down to give out branches, can you tell why?

> **Figure Out**
> Why do you think cities are built near the river bank?

confluence: a place where two rivers meet; estuary: the mouth of a large river, when the river enters the sea in one stream without branching into smaller streams; distributary: a branch of a river that flows out from the main river

Major rivers in India

The Mahanadi flows through the states of Madhya Pradesh and Odisha into the Bay of Bengal. The Krishna, Godavari and Kaveri also flow through the plateau region into the Bay of Bengal. The Brahmaputra rises in the Himalayas, flows through Assam and then into Bangladesh (where it is known as Jamuna), and finally enters the Bay of Bengal. Most of the rivers flow into the Bay of Bengal because the Indian landmass slopes eastwards.

Importance of rivers

Rivers play a very important role in the lives of the people. Nearly all the major cities of India are located by the banks of rivers. The rivers become the means of:

- potable water
- irrigation
- transportation
- livelihood
- electricity
- drainage

Rivers and their tributaries are the main channels of water supply in India. We must keep them clean.

In a Nutshell

- India is a land of rivers.
- The perennial rivers like Ganga and Mahanadi, have water throughout the year.
- The seasonal or non-perennial rivers get water only during the monsoons or rainy season.
- Ganga, Yamuna, and the Indus and its tributaries, flow through the Indian Gangetic Plain.
- The Narmada and Tapi flow into the Arabian Sea.
- The Mahanadi, Krishna and Kaveri are the rivers of the southern peninsula region.
- Rivers are channels of drainage and water supply in India. We must keep our rivers clean.

Workout

A. Fill in the blanks.

1. Rivers in India are channels of .... and ....
2. The .... rivers have water throughout the year.
3. A .... is built across the river to control its flow.
4. The .... Delta is the largest in the world.
5. .... rivers are those which do not have water throughout the year.

B. Match the columns.

	Column A		Column B
1.	Brahmaputra	a.	distributary of Ganga
2.	Hooghly	b.	flows into the Arabian Sea
3.	Triveni Sangam	c.	flows into the Bay of Bengal
4.	Narmada	d.	Jamuna
5.	Mahanadi	e.	Allahabad

C. Give one word for each.

1. The place from where rivers originate on mountains: ....
2. The river that joins a larger river: ....
3. A smaller river that branches out from the main river: ....
4. The river that enters the sea in one stream: ....

D. Answer these questions in brief.

1. Name two rivers that rise in the Himalayas.
2. Name a river that enters Bangladesh from India.
3. What do we call the place where two rivers meet?

E. Answer these questions in detail.

1. What is the difference between a perennial and a seasonal river?
2. List the tributaries of the Ganga.
3. Write a short note on the importance of rivers.

F. Map Work

On a blank political map of India, mark the following:

- major rivers in India
- one city located along their banks

Think Box

Why is Punjab called the land of five rivers?

Picture Study

Look at the picture and answer these question

1. Name the monument and the river along which it is built.
2. Do you think this river is clean?
3. Give one measure that can be taken to keep the river clean.

Life Skills and Values

Imagine you are in a place where the river is the main source of water supply. Once when rains are delayed, the river dries up and water becomes scarce. State three steps you can take to save water.

Enjoy

A. Make a chart on the rivers and dams of the Southern Plateau. Paste colourful pictures and write briefly about their location.

B. Find out about any tank or pond which is used to harvest rainwater near your area. Write the information on a sheet of paper.

Weblinks

For more information, visit
https://knowindia.gov.in/profile/rivers.php
https://www.nationalgeographic.org/encyclopedia/ganges-river-basin/?utm_source=BibblioRCM_Row
Last accessed on 31/July/2020

12 The Northern Mountains

Let's learn about...

- life in the states of Himachal Pradesh, Uttarakhand.
- life in the union territories of Jammu and Kashmir and Ladakh.

Key Terms

- Himalayas
- mountain pass
- vegetation
- pilgrimage sites

Reflect

Talk about the landscape and the vegetation of a hill station. Is it any different from the plains? If yes, how?

States and Union Territories of the Himalayan Region

Jammu and Kashmir, Ladakh, Himachal Pradesh, Uttarakhand, Sikkim, Meghalaya, Tripura, Mizoram, Manipur, Nagaland and Arunachal Pradesh are the union territories and states located in the Himalayan region. Some parts of West Bengal and Assam, especially the hilly areas, are also considered a part of the Himalayan mountain range.

FactPedia

The word Himalayas means the 'abode of snow' in Sanskrit.

Jammu and Kashmir

Jammu and Kashmir is one of the northernmost union territories of India. Jammu is its winter capital and Srinagar is the summer capital. The mountain ranges that pass through this region are the Karakoram range and the Pir Panjal Range. The Indus, Chenab, Sutlej and Jhelum are some of the important rivers of Jammu and Kashmir. The Jammu plains have a comparatively warmer climate. The mountain belt of Kashmir has very cold winters and warm summers.

Figure Out

Why does Jammu and Kashmir have two capitals?

Kashmir valley

The vegetation of this region depends on the altitude. It varies from evergreen cedar, pine and spruce trees

sparse: hardly any or very little

in the hillsides and chinar in the valleys to sparse vegetation. Crops like maize, rice, kidney beans (rajma) and vegetables are grown. Fruits such as apples, figs, plums, apricot, peaches, cherries, and nuts, such as walnuts and almonds grow in this region. Saffron, an aromatic spice obtained from a flower, is also grown in many parts of Kashmir.

> **FactPedia**
> A small clay pot with lighted coal, called *kangri*, is used in Kashmir by the people to keep themselves warm during the winters.

Handicrafts, furniture, woollen and silk carpets, embroidered shawls and paper mache are some of the famous products of Jammu and Kashmir.

Kashmir is a popular destination for tourists. Some tourists live in houseboats on the Dal Lake. The Dal Lake is famous for its scenic location, for its *shikaras* (boats) that float on it and also for its 'floating vegetable market'. Other places of interest are Gulmarg, Pahalgam, and the Wular Lake. Vaishno Devi and the Amarnath cave are places of religious importance. People speak Kashmiri in Kashmir and Dogri in Jammu. Many Kashmiris drink a local tea called *kehwa,* which is made in local tea urns called *samovars*. The most popular festivals are Maha Shivratri and Eid. The ***phiran***, a loose kurta for men and women, is the traditional dress of Kashmir.

Floating market in Kashmir

Ladakh

The union territory of Ladakh experiences an extremely cold and dry climate. Ladakh is the northernmost union territory in India. Ladakh is divided into two districts—Kargil and Leh. Its capital city is Leh. The rivers, Indus and Zanskar flow through the region. The mountain ranges in the region are Ladakh Range, the Zanskar Range and the Karakoram mountains. A pass in a mountain range is a natural passage for movement across the mountains. The Zoji la Pass and Nathu la Pass are used for movement of people and goods in Ladakh.

Leh, Ladakh

Ladakh is the highest plateau in India and has a desert type of climate. Due to its altitude, the region is a cold desert with very cold winters and pleasant summers. There is sparse vegetation as a result of scanty rainfall. People grow potatoes, barley, and fruits like apricots and walnuts. People here are mainly Buddhists. Ladakh is known for its monastries, valleys and lakes. People speak Ladakhi language.

altitude: the height above sea level

DIY

There are houseboats in Kashmir as well as in Kerala. Find out the similarities and differences between the houseboats of both the states.

Himachal Pradesh

A girl from Himachal Pradesh dressed in her traditional dress

Shimla is the state capital of Himachal Pradesh. The rivers Chenab, Sutlej, Beas and Ravi flow through this state. The climate in the hilly regions is very cold and they experience snowfall in the winter. The summers are pleasant.

Coniferous trees, such as the fir, spruce, pine, deodar and ferns, form the natural vegetation of the region. A variety of fruits like apples, pears, plums, cherries, apricots and peaches are grown in orchards. Maize, barley, rice and vegetables are also grown on the terraced hillsides. Himachal is famous for its Kullu shawls, waist coats and caps with colourful woven borders and motifs. The most important festival of the region is Dussehra.

People speak Hindi, Punjabi, Kinnauri and Pahari. Long robes, shawls and scarves are the traditional clothes of women. Men wear kurta pajamas, jackets and Himachali caps. Shimla, Kullu, Manali and Dalhousie are located here and are very popular holiday destinations for tourists.

Uttarakhand

Laxman Jhula bridge over the river Ganga

Uttarakhand is located on the southern side of the Himalayan range. Dehradun is its capital city. The highest regions of Uttarakhand are covered with snow and glaciers. The Gangotri glacier, which is the source of the river Ganga, and the Yamunotri glacier, which is the source of the river Yamuna, are both located in this state. The climate of this state varies according to the altitude. It ranges from very cold regions with snowfall to regions with a pleasant climate.

The vegetation in the colder regions is evergreen trees, such as pine, spruce, oak, cedar and chestnut. The sal, teak, shisham and dhak (palash) trees grow in the lower regions of Uttarakhand. Rhododendron trees are also common. Local handicrafts are made of wood. In the hilly regions, maize, barley and rice are grown on terraced fields. Fruits are also grown in some regions. People speak Hindi, Kumaoni, Garhwali and other Pahari languages.

Tourism is a very important industry in Uttarakhand. There are many pilgrimage sites like Rishikesh with its famous Laxman Jhula bridge, Badrinath, Kedarnath, Gangotri, Yamunotri and Hemkund Sahib. Hill stations like Ranikhet, Nainital, Mussoorie and Auli and the Valley of Flowers are popular tourist attractions.

Green Earth

Large-scale deforestation to build facilities for tourists in the Northern Himalayas has an adverse impact on the climate.

In a Nutshell

- Ladakh is the northernmost union territory in India, while Jammu and Kashmir is the other.
- Himachal Pradesh lies to the south of Jammu and Kashmir. Shimla, Kullu, Manali and Dalhousie are the popular holiday destinations of this state.
- Uttarakhand lies in the southern side of the Himalayan range. Badrinath, Kedarnath, Hemkund Saheb, Gangotri and Yamunotri are located in this state.

Workout

A. Tick the correct answers and fill in the blanks.

1. Rhododendron trees are common in .... (Uttarakhand/Rajasthan)
2. .... (Kehwa/Ice tea) is a local tea of Jammu and Kashmir.
3. Kinnauri language is spoken in .... (Srinagar/Himachal Pradesh).
4. Nathu la Pass is located in .... (Himachal Pradesh/Ladakh)

B. Fill in the blanks.

1. The people of Kashmir wear a traditional dress called ....
2. .... is the source of the river Ganga.
3. .... is another name for Palash tree.
4. .... is the summer capital city of Jammu and Kashmir.

pilgrimage sites: sacred places that people travel to as an act of religious devotion

C. Write T for true and F for false.

1. Papier mâché is a popular industry of Jammu and Kashmir. [ ]
2. Dogri is a language spoken in Ladakh. [ ]
3. Manali is the capital of Himachal Pradesh. [ ]
4. The Valley of Flowers is located in Uttarakhand. [ ]

D. Answer these questions in brief.

1. Which region is known as a cold desert in India?
2. Name two trees that grow in Himachal Pradesh.
3. Name two tourist destinations in Kashmir.

E. Answer these questions in detail.

1. What kind of crops and fruits grow in Kashmir?
2. Describe the vegetation of Uttarakhand.
3. Write a note on the location and people of Himachal Pradesh.

F. Map Work

On an outline physical map of India, mark the Himalayan mountain range, the states and the union territories of the Northern Mountain region. Make a key or a legend.

Think Box

Why do you think tourism is a very important industry in Uttarakhand?

Picture Study

Look at the picture and answer the questions that follow.

1. Identify the object shown in this picture.
2. What is it used for?
3. Name the region where it is used.

Life Skills and Values

Work in groups. Find out the names of the major festivals celebrated in the hilly states of the Himalayas. How are they celebrated?

Enjoy

Make a Walnut Fudge

Ingredients

- 100 grams of chocolate cake
- 4 walnut kernels
- 3 teaspoons unsalted butter
- 2 teaspoons icing sugar
- 1 teaspoon cocoa powder

Method

Cut the walnuts into small pieces. Keep them aside. Crumble the chocolate cake. Mix the butter, icing sugar and cocoa with the cake crumbs. Using your hands, make small balls from the mixture. Roll the balls over the crushed walnut kernels. The walnut fudge is ready to be eaten.

Weblinks

For more information, visit
https://himachaltourism.gov.in/great-himalayas/
OR
https://leh.nic.in/tourism/places-of-interest/
Last accessed on 31/July/2020

13 The Northeastern States

Let's learn about...

- the northeastern states.
- the climate.
- the vegetation.
- famous places to visit.

Key Terms

- Brahmaputra
- Tea plantation
- Naga hills
- Loktak lake
- Mawsynram

Reflect

Why do you think the states in northeastern India are called the seven sisters?

The Seven Sister states are the contiguous states of Arunachal Pradesh, Assam, Meghalaya, Manipur, Mizoram, Nagaland and Tripura in the northeastern part of India. In 2002, Sikkim was included as the eighth state of the northeastern region. These states are a part of the Northern Mountain range and they lie in the Purvanchal Range. Let us read more about these states.

The northeastern states of India

Arunachal Pradesh

Arunachal Pradesh is a hilly state. The river, Brahmaputra, enters India through this state. Itanagar is its capital. This state receives heavy rainfall. People living in the flood prone regions sometimes build houses on stilts to protect themselves from rain and floods. Farming and weaving are the main occupations of the people of Arunachal Pradesh. Wheat, paddy and maize are the main crops grown here. Many tourists visit this state for its natural

Green Earth

Deforestation in the hills for timber leads to landslides during heavy rains.

contiguous: next to something, neighbouring

DIY

Find out names of other states in India where people build houses on stilts.

FactPedia

The Tawang Monastery is the largest monastery in India and second largest in the world.

beauty. The Tawang Monastery and the Namdapha National Park are some of the famous places to visit in Arunachal Pradesh.

Assam

Assam is also known as the 'gateway to the northeast'. The Brahmaputra river flows through this state, making the land fertile. Dispur is the capital, but Guwahati is the largest city. Rice and jute are the main crops. Tea is grown in large areas called **tea plantations**. Assam tea is famous all over the world. The Assamese women wear a dress called Mekhela Chadar. Bihu is a folk dance from Assam.

One horned rhinoceros in Kaziranga

Assam has five national parks. Out of these, Kaziranga National Park is famous for its one horned rhinoceros and Manas National Park has a tiger and an elephant reserve. The Kamakhya temple in Guwahati is another tourist attraction. The state is known for its Muga silk and bamboo handicrafts.

Figure Out

Why is Assam known as the 'gateway to the northeast'?

Nagaland

Nagaland forms the international boundary of India with Myanmar. Located in the Naga hill range, this region has wet and cool climate. Its capital city is Kohima. Nagaland is home to many tribes. Each tribe wears a colourful shawl with unique designs. Farmers grow rice, maize, millets and potatoes. Weaving and woodwork are the other occupations. The Hornbill Festival, held in early winter, is a big tourist attraction.

Hornbill festival, Nagaland

Manipur

Loktak Lake, Manipur

Manipur shares its border with Myanmar. Loktak, the largest fresh water lake, is in the north-east of this state. The climate of the state is pleasant throughout the year except during the winter months when it is cold. Farming is an important occupation and rice is the most important crop. Tea, coffee, rubber, cardamom, fruits and vegetables are also grown. The famous classical Manipuri dance originated in this region. The capital of this state is Imphal.

Cheraw dance, Mizoram

Mizoram

Mizoram is a hilly state and it shares its boundaries with Myanmar and Bangladesh. Agriculture is the main occupation of the Mizos. It has one of the highest literacy rates in the country. The Mizos make a variety of bamboo products and handicrafts. Cheraw or the bamboo dance is a popular folk dance. Aizawl is the state capital.

Tripura

Tripura is surrounded by Bangladesh on three sides. Rice, pineapple and jute are the main crops grown in the state. Handicrafts are made from cane, bamboo and wood. Goria is a popular folk dance of Tripura. Agartala is the capital of the state. The Ujjayanta Palace in Agartala, which is the State Museum with an impressive collection of royal and cultural artefacts, is an important tourist attraction.

Ujjayanta Palace, Tripura

Nohkalikai Waterfall in Khasi hills, Meghalaya

Meghalaya

Meghalaya, the land of the Khasi, Garo and Jaintia Hills, shares its borders with Bangladesh. 'Meghalaya' means the abode of clouds. Mawsynram, a village in this state, has the heaviest rainfall in the world. Agriculture is an important occupation. Rice, maize, potatoes, pineapples, oranges and many other fruits are grown here. Shillong is the capital and is a popular tourist spot.

literacy rate: the number of people who are able to read and write

Sikkim

Sikkim is the eighth state of the northeastern region. Sikkim is bordered by Bhutan, Tibet and Nepal. It has cool summers and cold winters. It is a popular tourist destination. Farming and weaving are two major occupations. The red panda is found in this state. Gangtok is the capital of Sikkim.

The red panda, Sikkim

In a Nutshell

- The seven sister states are contiguous states.
- Sikkim is the eighth state of the northeastern region.
- Arunachal Pradesh is a hilly state.
- Assam is the gateway to the northeast by road. It has Kaziranga and Manas national parks.
- The Naga Hills are in Nagaland. The state also celebrates the famous Hornbill festival.
- The Manipuri dance is the famous classical dance from Manipur.
- Mizoram shares its international boundaries with Myanmar and Bangladesh.
- Tripura is surrounded by Bangladesh on three sides.
- Meghalaya has Khasi, Garo and Jaintia Hills.

Workout

A. Tick the correct answers and fill in the blanks.

1. The .... Hills are located in Meghalaya.
   a. Khasi b. Shivalik c. Naga
2. .... is a dance from Tripura.
   a. Cheraw b. Garba c. Goria
3. The wettest place in the world is ....
   a. Cherrapunji b. Mawsynram c. Itanagar
4. The state that is surrounded by Bangladesh on three sides is ....
   a. Mizoram b. Meghalaya c. Tripura

B. Fill in the blanks.

1. .... is the largest city in Assam.
2. The .... Monastery is in Arunachal Pradesh.
3. The Mekhela Chadar is the traditional dress of ....
4. .... is the eighth state to be included as part of the northeastern region.

C. Match the columns.

	Column A		Column B
1.	Meghalaya	a.	Hornbill festival
2.	Nagaland	b.	Garo Hills
3.	Assam	c.	Loktak Lake
4.	Manipur	d.	Bihu

D. Answer these questions in brief.

1. What is the main occupation of the Mizos? What is their popular folk dance called?
2. Why are houses in Arunachal Pradesh built on stilts?
3. Describe the climate of Manipur.

E. Answer these questions in detail.

1. List the national parks of Assam with the animals found in them.
2. Write a note on Nagaland.
3. Write a note on Sikkim.

F. Map Work

On a blank political map of India, mark and colour the eight north eastern states. Then mark their capital cities. Make a key.

Think Box

A. Most of the states in the northeast are hilly. How do people travel in these places?

B. Mizoram has one of the highest literacy rates in the country. Why do you think that is so?

Picture Study

Look at the picture of the Living Roots Bridge and answer the question.

1. Which state has this kind of bridge?
2. Why do you think they are called so?

Life Skills and Values

In groups, list the tourist attractions for each of the seven sister states and create a brochure for the tourists.

Enjoy

A. Find out one popular dish from any one northeastern state. Write down the recipe and share it with your classmates.

B. Collect bamboo strips with the help of an adult. Make any craft item like a wall hanging, a coaster, jewellery, a picture frame or a pencil holder with them.

Weblinks

For more information, visit
http://northeasttourism.gov.in/
Last accessed on 31/July/2020

14 The Northern Plains and the Desert Region

Let's learn about...

- culture of the region.
- important cities of the Northern Plains.
- the states in the desert region.

Key Terms

- Northern Plains
- West Bengal
- Bihar
- Haryana
- Punjab
- Uttar Pradesh
- National Capital Region
- The Desert Region
- Rajasthan
- Banjaras
- Gujarat

Reflect

Using an atlas, find out the names of the states through which these rivers flow.

- Indus: ....
- Ganga: ....
- Brahmaputra: ....

Let us learn about some of the states of the Northern Plains.

Punjab

Punjab is a state situated in the northwestern part of India. Chandigarh is the common capital for Punjab and Haryana. The word 'Punjab' means 'a land of five rivers'. The rivers Ravi, Sutlej and Beas, flow through the state. Chenab and Jhelum are the other two rivers.

FactPedia

The state animal of Punjab is the blackbuck and the state bird is the goshawk.

The climate in Punjab is very cold in winter and hot and dry in summer. The soil is fertile and many crops, such as wheat, rice, sugarcane and mustard, grow here. Agriculture, dairy farming and poultry farming are important occupations of the people in Punjab. Some of the most delicious food items of Punjab are *sarson ka saag* with *makki ki roti*, and paratha with white butter and *lassi*. Baisakhi and Lohri are the important festivals celebrated here.

Golden Temple, Amritsar

The important cities of Punjab are Ludhiana, Amritsar and Jalandhar. The famous Golden Temple is situated in Amritsar. Most people living in Punjab speak Punjabi. Bhangra and Gidda are the famous dances that originated in Punjab. Phulkari is the traditional embroidery of Punjab.

Figure Out

What is the significance of the festivals of Baisakhi, Teej and Lohri?

Haryana

Gurugram, Haryana

Haryana is a state in the north-central region of India. The land here is flat and fertile. It has dry hot climate in the summer season, and the winters are cold. Canals have been built to bring water from different rivers to irrigate the land. The main crops grown here are wheat, rice and cotton. The state also produces sugarcane, mustard seeds, corn and potato.

There are many important cities and towns in Haryana. Gurugram, which is an important industrial hub of India, is situated in this state. Other places of importance are Faridabad, an industrial town, Ambala and Karnal. Kurukshetra and Panipat are places of historical importance and attract many tourists. The main occupation of the people in Haryana is agriculture. Other industries are farm machines and tractor manufacturing, cotton and sugar industries. Haryana is also famous for its dairy products.

Delhi

Rajpath leading to India Gate, Delhi

The National Capital Territory (NCT) of Delhi is bound by Haryana in the north, west and south and Uttar Pradesh in the east. New Delhi is the national capital of India. It is located in north-central India. It is a part of the National Capital Region (NCR) which also comprises some parts of Haryana, Uttar Pradesh and Rajasthan.

Delhi is both a union territory and a state. It is governed by a lieutenant governor who is assisted by a chief minister. The president and the prime minister of India reside in New Delhi. The president lives in the Rashtrapati Bhavan. The prime minister and his cabinet of ministers meet in the Parliament House or Sansad Bhavan.

hub: centre or the most important part of a place or an activity

There are many important offices in and around Delhi. A large number of people from the other states of India come to Delhi to live and work. Many monuments in Delhi attract tourists from all over the world. Some of these important historical places are the Red Fort, India Gate, Qutub Minar, Humayun's Tomb, Rajghat, Jantar Mantar, Jama Masjid and the Akshardham Temple.

Delhi experiences an extreme climate which is very hot in summer and cold in winter. Wheat and many vegetables are grown here. Hindi is the most popular language spoken in Delhi.

Chandigarh

Rock Garden, Chandigarh

Chandigarh is a union territory as well as a city. It is the capital city of both Haryana and Punjab. It is a very well planned city where the straight roads divide it into sectors forming a grid. Each sector has its own hospital, educational institutions, parks, markets and shopping malls. Chandigarh is very hot in summers and very cold in winters. Most of Chandigarh is covered with dense banyan and eucalyptus plantations. The Rock Garden and the Rose Garden are famous tourist spots.

Uttar Pradesh

Ganga river, Varanasi

Uttar Pradesh is the most thickly populated state of India. Lucknow is its capital. The Ganga, Yamuna, Gomti, Ghaghara, Betwa and Chambal rivers flow through the state. The climate in Uttar Pradesh is generally warm with the rainy season lasting from June to September. The land here is flat and fertile. The natural vegetation includes grasslands and forests. Major crops such as wheat, rice, sugarcane and maize are grown. The state also produces delicious varieties of mangoes known as *dasheri and langra.*

Agra and Kanpur are some of the important cities of Uttar Pradesh. The famous Taj Mahal is situated in Agra and it attracts tourists from all over the world. Kanpur is famous for textile, chemicals, leather and engineering industries. Kathak, a famous classical dance, originated in Uttar Pradesh. Uttar Pradesh is famous for its handicrafts such as silk sarees—the

FactPedia

Uttar Pradesh is famous for producing a delicious cuisine from Lucknow known as Awadhi cuisine.

brocade designs of Varanasi, the *chikan* embroidery of Lucknow, the carpentry in Saharanpur and the brass work of Moradabad. Hindi and Urdu are the dominant spoken languages of Uttar Pradesh.

Bihar

Bihar lies in the eastern part of India. It is bordered by Nepal in the north, West Bengal in the east, Uttar Pradesh in the west and Jharkhand in the south. Patna is the capital of Bihar. The major rivers flowing through the state are the Ganga, Gandak, Kosi and Son rivers. Bihar has a warm climate with monsoons in July-August.

Bodh Gaya

As the state has many rivers, the fertile soil is used for the cultivation of crops, such as rice, sugarcane and vegetables. Rice, pulses and vegetables form the staple food of Bihar. *Litti choka* is one of the most famous dishes of Bihar. Bihar is famous for Madhubani paintings. The people here also make cane and bamboo articles and durries. Bhagalpur is famous for its fine quality silk.

Bihar has many places of historical importance, which attract a lot of tourists. Gautama Buddha spent many years, living and preaching in Bodh Gaya. Nalanda, an ancient Buddhist monastery, is a centre of learning since ancient times.

West Bengal

West Bengal is situated in the eastern part of India. The state has a unique location with the Himalayas in the north and the Bay of Bengal in the south. Kolkata, the capital of West Bengal, is situated on the east bank of the river, Hooghly, which is a distributary of the river Ganga. Howrah Bridge, which is a huge steel bridge, is constructed over the Hooghly river. The Ganges, flowing into the Bay of Bengal along with the river Brahmaputra, forms the Sundarbans delta, which is home to the Royal Bengal Tigers.

Howrah bridge, Kolkata

West Bengal is one of the largest producers of rice and jute in India. The hilly areas in the north are famous for producing fine quality tea. Wheat, potatoes and mangoes are

carpentry: the skill of making furniture such as chairs, tables, etc.; durries: heavy cotton rugs from India; preaching: to give a talk in a public place; monastery: a place where monks live and teach; distributary: a branch of a river that moves away from the main river

also cultivated here. Rice and fish are the staple food of West Bengal. The state is also famous for its sweets, rasgulla and sandesh. West Bengal is also famous for the beautiful hand-embroidered *kantha* work which is done on silk and cotton fabrics. Bengali is the main language spoken in West Bengal.

A busy street in Kolkata

Kolkata is known as the 'city of joy'. The places of tourist interest are the Victoria Memorial, Botanical Gardens and the Kalighat Kali Temple. Shantiniketan, a famous university was set up by the renowned poet, Rabindranath Tagore here. Kolkata was the first city to have an underground metro rail system in India. It is the only city to have trams as a means of transport. Mother Teresa spent her life serving the poor in this city. Darjiling, a hill station in the north of West Bengal, also attracts tourists.

Figure Out

Find out the name of the organization set up by Mother Teresa.

DIY

Fill in the table given below by choosing any three states lying in the Northern Plains.

Name of the state	Crops grown	Vegetation

The Desert Region

The Thar Desert

The Great Indian Desert is also known as the Thar Desert. It stretches from the Rann of Kutch in Gujarat to the borders of Haryana. A large part of Rajasthan lies in the Thar Desert.

Rajasthan

Rajasthan, known as the 'desert state', is located in the northwestern part of India. The capital of this land of forts, is the Pink City of Jaipur. The climate in this region is very hot and dry in summers and very cold in winters. While temperatures are high during the day, the nights are always cool. Agriculture, sheep rearing, textile printing, tourism and handicrafts are the main occupations of the people of Rajasthan. Farmers grow chillies, bajra and oilseeds. Due to the scarcity of water, people sometimes move in groups from one place to another searching for water. These people are called banjaras. The people of Rajasthan speak Hindi and Rajasthani. Jaisalmer, Jodhpur, Pushkar and Chittorgarh with their famous forts are some of the important tourist places in Rajasthan.

Amer Fort, Jaipur

Gujarat

The state of Gujarat lies in western India. Gandhinagar is its capital. Farming is the main occupation of the people. The crops grown here are *jowar*, *bajra*, cotton, oilseeds, sugarcane and wheat. The Rann of Kutch region in this state is known for its embroidered clothes with mirror work. The desert region is also known for animals like the wild ass and the desert fox. Somnath Temple, Dwarka, Junagadh Fort, Akshar Dham, Gir National Park, Sabarmati Ashram are some of the tourist places in this state.

The mirror work of Gujarat

Green Earth

The clearing of forests and overgrazing is increasing the spread of desert land.

In a Nutshell

- The Northern Plains extend between the south of the Himalayas to the north of the Deccan Plateau.
- The states located in the Northern Plains are Punjab, Haryana, Delhi, Uttar Pradesh, Bihar and West Bengal.
- The Northern Plains have many navigable rivers that are suitable for both irrigation and transportation.
- The Great Indian Desert, or the Thar Desert, stretches from the Rann of Kutch in Gujarat to the borders of Haryana.
- Rajasthan and Gujarat are located in the Great Indian Desert region.

Workout

A. Fill in the blanks with the correct answers.

1. .... in Uttar Pradesh is famous for *chikan* work. (Kanpur/Lucknow)
2. .... is a distributary of the river Ganga. (Hooghly/Yamuna)
3. Gurugram is located in .... (Delhi/Haryana)
4. The .... Desert stretches from the Rann of Kutch in Gujarat to the borders of Haryana. (Sahara/Thar)

B. Match the columns.

	Column A		**Column B**
1.	Bihar	a.	rasgulla
2.	Uttar Pradesh	b.	chillies
3.	West Bengal	c.	litti choka
4.	Punjab	d.	langra
5.	Rajasthan	e.	sarson ka saag

C. Answer in one word.

1. A famous dance of Punjab: ....
2. A famous painting style of Bihar: ....
3. The famous hand embroidery from West Bengal: ....
4. Rajghat is located here: ....
5. The capital city of both Haryana and Punjab: ....

D. Answer these questions in brief.

1. Name the important industries of Haryana.
2. Name two important cities of Uttar Pradesh. What are they famous for?
3. Name a place of historical importance in Bihar.
4. What kind of crops are grown in the state of Gujarat?

E. Answer these questions in detail.

1. Explain the importance of the Northern Plains.
2. Write a short note on the important places in West Bengal.
3. Why are some people in Rajasthan called 'banjaras'?
4. Write a short note on the National Capital Territory of Delhi.

Think Box

The Northern Plains have a good network of roads and railways. Why?

Picture Study

Look at the pictures and answer the questions.

1. Name the states located in the Northern Plains.
2. What is the difference between the climate of the Northern Plains and the Desert region?
3. Name two crops that can be grown in these two regions.

Life Skills and Values

Have an 'India Day' presentation.

Work in groups. Each group will represent a state from the Northern Plains and the Desert Region. Members of each group may wear the regional dresses, bring food and say something in the language of the state they are representing. Members of each group must also highlight one problem of their chosen state, such as scarcity of water, less rainfall or floods and suggest one way to tackle it.

Enjoy

A. Make a Travel Brochure

With the help of an atlas, find the names of cities you would like to visit in the Northern Plains. Select one city from each state and write a short note on it. Collect pictures and information from the internet. Make a PowerPoint presentation and present it in the classroom.

B. Find out the different ways in which people greet one another in the different states of the Northern Plains and write these down.

Weblinks

For more information, visit
https://www.incredibleindia.org/content/incredible-india-v2/en/experiences/art.html
https://www.incredibleindia.org/content/incredible-india-v2/en/experiences/heritage/most-popular.html
Last accessed on 31/July/2020

15 The Peninsular Region and the Islands

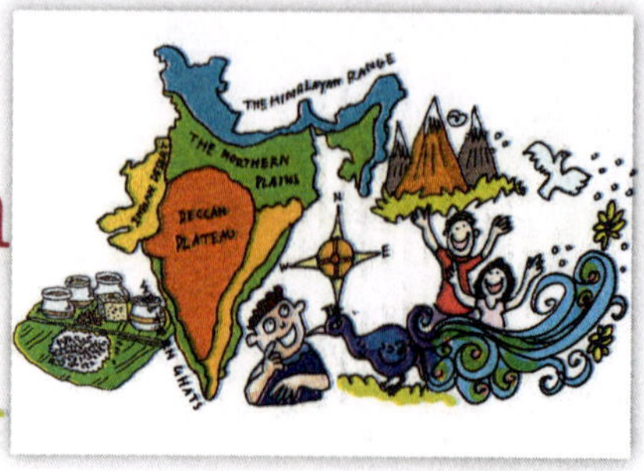

Let's learn about...

- the Peninsular Plateau and Island Regions.
- life in the states of these regions.

Key Terms

- Eastern Ghats
- Metur Dam
- Hirakud
- Khajuraho
- Western Ghats
- Chota Nagpur Plateau
- Thanjavur
- island region

Reflect

Both plateaus and plains are flatlands. Discuss the difference between them.

Let us learn about the states located in the Peninsular Plateau region.

Madhya Pradesh

Kanha Tiger Reserve

Madhya Pradesh is a large state located in central India. Bhopal is its capital city. Gwalior, Indore and Jabalpur are other important cities of the state. River Narmada, Tapi, Chambal, Son and Betwa flow through this state. The vegetation consists of thick forests. Farmers cultivate cotton and wheat in this region. The Pachmahri hill station, Kanha Tiger Reserve and Bandhavgarh National Park are some of the places of interest in Madhya Pradesh. The temples of **Khajuraho** are important monuments. The diamond mines at Panna are also located in this state.

Chhattisgarh

Chitrakote waterfalls

Chhattisgarh is located in east-central India. Raipur is its capital city. This state is mainly located along the Mahanadi river basin. Indravati, Arpa and Pairi are some of the important rivers. The state experiences hot, dry and windy summers, heavy rainfall during the rainy season and pleasant winters.

The state is rich in minerals, such as coal, iron and bauxite. Mining, agriculture, energy production and manufacturing are the main industries of Chhattisgarh. The major crops grown here are rice and maize. The Chitrakote waterfalls, Bhoramdeo temple, Danteshwari Devi temple and Tirathgarh waterfalls are famous places to visit in Chattisgarh. Indravati National Park is the only tiger reserve of this state.

Jharkhand

Jharkhand is located in the northeastern part of India. Ranchi is its capital. Most of Jharkhand falls under the Chota Nagpur Plateau. Jharkhand is almost entirely covered by plateaus, hills and valleys. The two main plateaus are Hazaribagh and Ranchi. They are separated by the river Damodar. The Subarnarekha, the Brahmani and the Son are the other rivers that run through the state.

Coal mining in Jharkhand

Jharkhand has a huge forest cover. Jharkhand has the largest coal reserves in India and Dhanbad has many coal mines. Jamshedpur, Bokaro and Ranchi are important industrial towns known for steel production. The state grows many crops, like rice, wheat and pulses.

Odisha

Odisha is located in northeastern India. Bhubaneswar is its capital city. Cuttack and Puri are the other big towns. Paradip is an important port. The famous Jagannath temple is in Puri where the annual Rath Yatra is held.

Lake Chilka

Odisha is known for its silver work called 'filigree' and textiles. Ricc and jute are the main crops grown. The Hirakud Dam is built on the Mahanadi river that flows through this state. The classical dance, Odissi, belongs to this state. The famous Lake Chilka, a home for migratory birds lies along the coastal plain.

Maharashtra

Maharashtra extends from the Sahyadri range to the western sea coast. Mumbai is the capital. Other important towns are Nagpur, Pune, Aurangabad and Nasik. The Godavari and Krishna rivers flow through this state. This state is one of the largest producers of cotton in India.

Mumbai skyline

Other crops like sugarcane, grapes and banana are also grown. Alphonso mango and oranges from Nagpur are famous fruits of the region. People speak Marathi language. The most popular festival of this state is Ganesh Chaturthi. The tourist attractions are the Ajanta and Ellora Caves, Elephanta Caves, Mahabaleshwar and Panchgani. The state has many important industries like automobiles, textiles and electronics. The Indian film industry, Bollywood, is in Mumbai.

Goa

Goa lies on the south western coast of India along the Arabian Sea. It is the smallest state in India. Panaji is the capital of this state. Other important cities are Marmagaon, Madgaon. The climate is generally hot and humid with frequent rainfall. People speak Konkani language. Major crops grown here are rice, legumes and ragi.

A beach in Goa

People also grow cashewnut, sugarcane, coconut, pineapples and mangoes. Fishing and tourism are the main occupations. Goa is an important tourist destination and is famous for its white sandy beaches. The beautiful churches and sanctuaries attract many tourists from all over the world.

Dadra and Nagar Haveli and Daman and Diu

The union territory of Daman and Diu and Dadra and Nagar Haveli has four important cities. Daman and Diu are separated by the Gulf of Khambat. While Daman is a coastal town in western India, Diu is an island. Daman is the capital of this region. Being a coastal region, fishing and working in coconut plantations are the major occupations. Both Daman and Diu were old Portuguese colonies and many buildings here have Portuguese style of architecture. Dadra and Nagar Haveli were also formerly Portuguese colonies. The presence of the Western Ghats makes the place hilly but it is flat in the central area. The river Daman Ganga flows through this region.

FactPedia

On 3 December, 2019, the Indian government merged the union territories of Dadra and Nagar Haveli and Daman and Diu into one administrative unit.

Karnataka

Karnataka lies to the south of Maharashtra. Bengaluru is the capital. Other important towns are Mysore, Hubli and Bijapur. The rivers, Krishna and Kaveri,

Mysore Palace

flow through this state. Teak and sandalwood trees grow here in abundance and many products are made from them. Farmers grow cotton, sugarcane, coffee and spices.

Bengaluru is the hub of software and IT industries. There are many other industries like aircraft manufacturing, electronic goods and automobiles. The language spoken is Kannada. The tourist attractions are the Mysore Palace, Brindavan Gardens, Jog Falls, as well as many temples. Dussehra and Ugadi are the popular festivals of the state.

Andhra Pradesh and Telangana

In 2014, the state of Andhra Pradesh was divided into two states—Andhra Pradesh and Telangana. The state capital is Hyderabad for the state of Telangana and also for Andhra Pradesh. However, Amaravati is now being prepared to become the official capital of Andhra Pradesh. The Krishna and Godavari rivers flow through this region. The Nagarjuna Dam is built on the river Krishna. The crops grown are cotton, jowar, groundnuts and tobacco. Most people speak Telugu and some people speak Urdu. The classical dance, Kuchipudi, is from the state of Andhra Pradesh. The major tourist attractions are the Salarjung Museum, the Charminar, Faluknama Palace, Film City and the Balaji Temple in Tirupati.

Kuchipudi

Kerala

Kerala is a state that lies along the south western coast of India, bordered by the Arabian Sea. Its capital is Thiruvananthapuram. Cochin is an important port town. It is a popular tourist destination and houses the famous Guruvayur Temple and the backwaters. People speak Malayalam. Tea, coffee, spices and rubber are grown here. Kathakali, a classical dance form, is from Kerala.

The Kerala backwaters

Tamil Nadu

Tamil Nadu lies in the southernmost part of the Indian peninsula. The state capital is Chennai. Other important towns are Madurai, Tiruchirappalli, Thanjavur and Kanchipuram. This state is famous for Kanjivaram silk sarees. Weaving and textiles are important industries of this state. Farmers grow rice, cotton, sugarcane and groundnuts. Tea and coffee are grown on the slopes of the Nilgiri Hills. Pongal

Shore Temple, Mahabalipuram

is an important festival of this region. Bharatanatyam, a famous classical dance form, is from this state. The Metur Dam is built on the river, Kaveri. The popular South Indian dishes like idli, dosa, upma and sambhar are the commonly eaten local food items of the state. The local language is Tamil. Some of the tourist attractions are the Meenakshi Temple in Madurai, the Brihadeshwara temple in Thanjavur, the Shore temple in Mahabalipuram and the Marina Beach in Chennai.

Figure Out

What is the importance of Metur Dam?

DIY

Find out more about the most visited tourist destination in each state located in the Peninsular Plateau. Paste the pictures on a big chart paper and write one sentence about each of them.

Puducherry

Puducherry is a union territory in the southern part of the Indian peninsula. It was formerly known as Pondicherry. The capital is also the city of Puducherry. It was once a French colony hence one can see few old settlements. The region has lovely beaches, churches, temples and the Aurobindo Ashram which are popular tourist places.

Green Earth

The Ministry of Housing and Urban Affairs, Government of India, has declared Indore as the cleanest city in 2020.

The Island Regions

A number of islands surround the Indian peninsula. Of these, the two biggest group of islands are the Andaman and Nicobar Islands and the Lakshadweep Islands.

Andaman and Nicobar Islands

The Andaman and Nicobar Islands are situated in the Bay of Bengal. The Andaman Islands are located in the north and the Nicobar Islands are in the south. Port Blair is the capital city. The southernmost tip of these islands is called Indira Point. The archipelago has over 500 islands, but only less than 40 are inhabited. Crops like rice, coconut and areca nuts are grown. Many tribal people still live on these islands and they do not like to be disturbed by tourists. The famous Cellular Jail (Kala Pani), where prisoners were kept during the British Raj, is in the Andamans. These islands are covered with forests. There are many sanctuaries and national parks that are great tourist attractions.

archipelago: a group of islands; inhabited: lived in

Lakshadweep Islands

The Lakshadweep Islands are situated in the Arabian Sea. It is a group of about forty coral islands. Coconut grows in abundance on these islands. Kavaratti is the capital. Fishing and tourism are the main occupations of the people. There are many tribal communities who have their own language and customs. Malayalam is also spoken in this region.

A beach in the Lakshadweep Islands

In a Nutshell

- Madhya Pradesh is a large state located in central India.
- Chhattisgarh and Jharkhand are mineral-rich states in the Peninsular Plateau region.
- Karnataka, Tamil Nadu, Kerala and Puducherry are the other states of this region.
- The Andaman and Nicobar Islands and the Lakshadweep Islands are the island regions of India.

Workout

A. Fill in the blanks.

1. The Bandhavgarh National Park is located in ....
2. The capital of Kerala is ....
3. The Hirakud Dam is built on the .... river.
4. The .... islands are situated in the Arabian Sea.

B. Match the columns.

	Column A		Column B
1.	Marmagaon	a.	Jharkhand
2.	Raipur	b.	Odisha
3.	Aurobindo Ashram	c.	Goa
4.	Lake Chilka	d.	Chhattisgarh
5.	Ranchi	e.	Puducherry

C. Write T for true and F for false.

1. Jharkhand is located along the Mahanadi river basin. ☐
2. The state with the largest coal reserves is Goa. ☐
3. Kuchipudi dance is from the state of Andhra Pradesh. ☐
4. Pongal is a festival celebrated in Tamil Nadu. ☐
5. The famous Cellular Jail (Kala Pani) is located in the Lakshadweep Islands. ☐

D. Answer these questions in brief.

1. Name the boundaries of the Southern Plateau.
2. Name the capital city or cities of Andhra Pradesh and Telangana.
3. Write a short note on Dadra and Nagar Haveli and Daman and Diu.
4. Name three tourist attractions of the state of Tamil Nadu.

E. Answer these questions in detail.

1. Write a short note on Madhya Pradesh.
2. Write a short note on the mineral-rich states of India.
3. Why are Goa and Kerala important tourist destinations?
4. Write a note on the island regions of India.

F. Map Work

Using an atlas, on an outline map of India, mark and label the following:

- Ghats: Eastern and Western
- Hill Ranges: Nilgiri, Satpura, Vindhya, Aravalli
- Rivers: Narmada, Tapi, Mahanadi, Godavari, Krishna, Kaveri
- Plateaus: Deccan, Malwa, Chota Nagpur
- Cities: Mumbai, Bengaluru, Chennai, Bhubaneshwar, Bhopal
- Islands: Andaman and Nicobar, Lakshadweep

Think Box

A mineral is an important raw material for many industries. Which industries will be affected if the mineral supply is exhausted?

Picture Study

Look at the picture and answer the questions.

1. Identify this temple.
2. Where is it located?

Life Skills and Values

A. A tourist would like to visit Maharashtra and Karnataka. Name a few tourist destinations they should visit during their trip.

B. Why does the state of Karnataka have extensive hydroelectric power? What will happen if suddenly the supply stops for three days?

Enjoy

A. There are eight classical dance forms in India. Four are mentioned in this lesson. Name them. Find out about the others. Make charts in groups describing each dance form.

B. Make an information brochure for the Island regions.

- the map of the region
- how to get there
- the climate
- the people and language spoken
- tourist spots
- things to do

Weblinks

For more information, visit
https://www.incredibleindia.org/content/incredible-india-v2/en/experiences/crafted-in-india/made-to-wear.html
https://lakshadweep.gov.in/about-lakshadweep/fauna-flora/
Last accessed on 31/July/2020

16 The Diversity of India

Let's learn about...

- the population of India.
- the languages of India.
- the festivals of India.
- the food and clothes of India.
- unity in diversity in India.

Key Terms

- diversity
- culture
- population
- traditional dress
- languages
- script

Reflect

Answer these questions.

1. What is your mother tongue? ....
2. Do you speak any other language? ....
3. What is the famous food of the state you live in? ....
4. What is the main festival celebrated in the state you live in? ....

India is a vast country with a large population. People live in different states, speak in varied languages, follow different religions, eat a variety of food and celebrate many festivals. All these together form the culture of India. Despite these differences, India is a land of unity in diversity.

Don't you wonder what is it that makes the people of 28 states and 8 union territories unite as Indians?

It is India's diverse population, languages, festivals, food and clothes that coexist to bring unity. Let us see how.

High rise buildings in a city

Population

Population means the number of people living in a place. India is the second-most populous country in the world.

populous: having a large population

The population is not distributed evenly throughout the states. Fewer people live in the mountainous and the desert regions, making them thinly populated. Many people live in the plains hence these regions are said to be densely populated.

Languages

People in India speak different languages. There are 22 languages mentioned in the Constitution of India. Some of these are Hindi, Marathi, Punjabi, Tamil, Urdu, Bengali, Assamese, Sindhi and Gujarati. The central government uses Hindi and English as the official languages. All states of India have a state language. Some languages, such as Hindi, are spoken by many people, while some languages are spoken only by a few people. Some languages are only spoken languages and do not have a script. They are mostly written in the Devanagari, English and Urdu scripts.

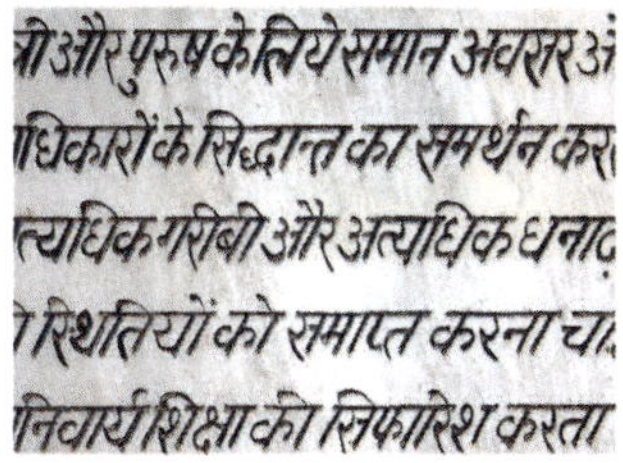

Devanagari script

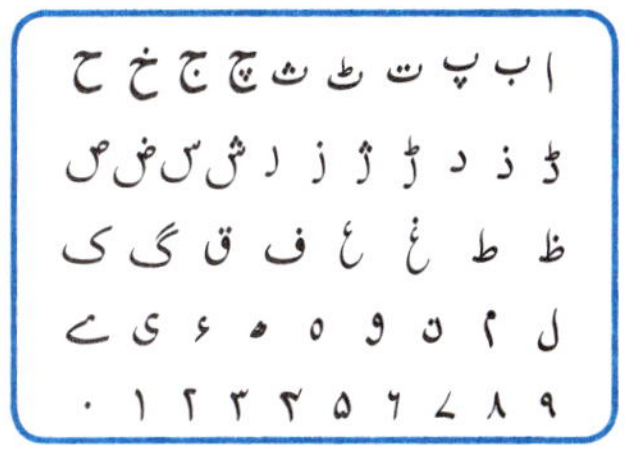

Urdu script

Festivals

People of every region celebrate different kinds of festivals. Festivals are a time for celebration, joy and sharing. They bring communities together and strengthen the bonds among them. We all love to dress up, eat special food, and have fun together during festivals. We have already learnt about the national festivals we celebrate in India. Some festivals are regional. For instance, Durga Puja and Saraswati Puja are mostly celebrated in Bengal, Ganesh Chaturthi in Maharashtra and Chhath Puja in Bihar and Jharkhand. Some of the harvest festivals that we celebrate are Baisakhi in Punjab, Pongal in Tamil Nadu and Bihu in Assam. Onam, Navroz, Gudi Padwa, Poila Boishakh are all names for the New Year celebrations of different communities in India.

FactPedia

The dates of some festivals are decided according to the position of the moon. These are called lunar festivals.

Food

People across India eat different kinds of food. A staple diet includes the food that is eaten regularly and in large quantities in a specific region. The climate and soil of a region determine the main crop that grows there. Rice is the staple food of the people living in the coastal, southern and eastern regions of India. Wheat is more popular in the northern states, while millets (jowar and bajra) are popular in the drier regions like Rajasthan and Gujarat. Dals or pulses are eaten throughout the country. A variety of fruits and vegetables grow throughout the year. On special occasions, certain sweets or special dishes are made. Pickles and preserves are eaten throughout the country.

evenly: equally; script: a set of letters in which a language is written; Devanagari: the alphabet used to write Sanskrit, Hindi and some other Indian languages; preserves: a type of food that can be eaten over a period of time because it does not go bad

India has different types of cuisines

Green Earth

We get food from plants and animals. If the environment is clean, then our food will also be clean and healthy.

Clothes

India experiences varied climatic conditions. In the mountain regions like Ladakh, it is very cold throughout the year. The southern regions are warm throughout the year. People dress according to the weather of a certain place. Synthetic and nylon clothes are also worn in some climates. The saree is the most common dress for women in India. Salwar kameez, churidar kurta and ghagras are the other Indian dresses. Men mostly wear kurta pajamas, dhotis, lungis, trousers and shirts. There are some clothes worn by both men and women like trousers, jeans, shirts, jackets and coats in most parts of the country. Each state has a traditional dress. People wear the traditional clothes during festivals, weddings and on special occasions.

Look at some of the traditional dresses worn in different states of India.

Kerala

Meghalaya

Jammu and Kashmir

Unity in Diversity

India is a vast country. The Constitution of India promises equality to everyone. All rules apply uniformly to all the people of India. All Indians have equal rights and certain duties towards their country. The national symbols and the national anthem of India remind us to respect one another. Even though people follow varied traditions and customs, they are all unified as citizens of the same nation.

Figure Out

Find out the different ways in which we greet one another in different states of India.

DIY

Look at the picture and answer these questions.

1. What do you think this picture depicts?
2. Do you think these children belong to different states in India?

In a Nutshell

- India is a diverse country.
- India is the second-most populous country in the world.
- The Constitution of India contains 22 languages.
- National, harvest and religious festivals are celebrated all over India.
- Each state has a traditional dress.
- All Indians have equal rights and certain duties towards their country.

Workout

A. Fill in the blanks.

1. .... is the most common dress worn by women in India.
2. A .... is a set of letters in which a language is written.
3. .... and .... are official languages for correspondence in India.
4. People wear .... clothes on special occasions.

B. Write T for true and F for false.

1. The population of India is growing rapidly. ☐
2. All languages have a script. ☐
3. All the people in India speak the same language. ☐
4. Rice is a staple diet for the people in the desert region. ☐

C. Match the columns.

Column A	Column B
1. Chhath Puja	a. Punjab
2. Saraswati Puja	b. Maharashtra
3. Ganesh Chaturthi	c. Assam
4. Baisakhi	d. Bengal
5. Bihu	e. Bihar

D. Answer these questions in brief.

1. What is meant by population?
2. What is a staple diet?
3. List the names of four new year festivals celebrated in India.
4. Name some clothes that both men and women wear in India.

E. Answer these questions in detail.

1. Why are festivals important?
2. Write a note on languages of India.
3. The staple diet of Indians varies from region to region. Comment and give examples.
4. What is unity in diversity?

Think Box

What would life be like if all the people in India followed the same religion, spoke one language, wore similar clothes, celebrated the same festival and ate the same food?

Picture Study

Look at the picture and answer the questions.

1. Name the food item seen here.
2. This food is the staple food of which state?
3. Which crop is used to make this food?
4. Name three states where this crop is cultivated.

Life Skills and Values

India is said to be a land of diversity. Yet, we are all united as Indians. Write down three things that show this unity.

Enjoy

A. Divide yourself in five groups. Choose five states. Find out the names of the special dishes, festivals and traditional dresses worn by people in those states. Collect pictures and make a collage.

B. Find out the recipe of a special dish. Prepare it at home with the help of your parents or grandparents. Bring it to school in the next class and share it with your classmates.

Weblinks

For more information, visit
https://www.incredibleindia.org/content/incredible-india-v2/en/experiences/food-and-cuisine.html
Last accessed on 31/July/2020

Across the Boundary 3

Map Scale

Look at the map scale and calculate the distance between the following by using a ruler.

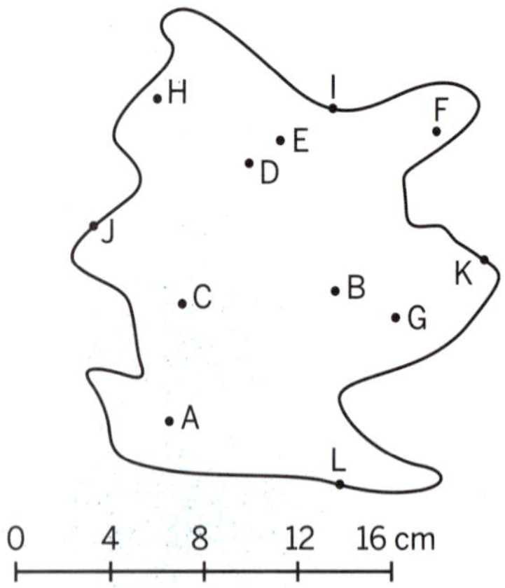

1. C and F:
2. B and H:
3. A and I:
4. K to E and then to D:
5. Total distance from A to J:
6. If each cm stands for 10 km, what is the actual distance from A to J?

Creative Skills

A group of travellers want to visit your state. Write a few lines about the tourist destinations in your state. You may paste some pictures too.

Be a Patriot

Write down the original and the English translation of the Indian National Anthem 'Jana Gana Mana'. Appreciate and understand the meaning and sing it with your friends at the end of the period. Do not forget to stand in attention position when you do so.

Connect with History

The Northern Plains of India was the area for the growth of early urban civilizations. Can you name the civilizations that flourished in the Indo-Gangetic Plains?

Map Skills

1. Which part of India does this picture show?
2. Name the seas on the western side and the eastern side of this part of India.

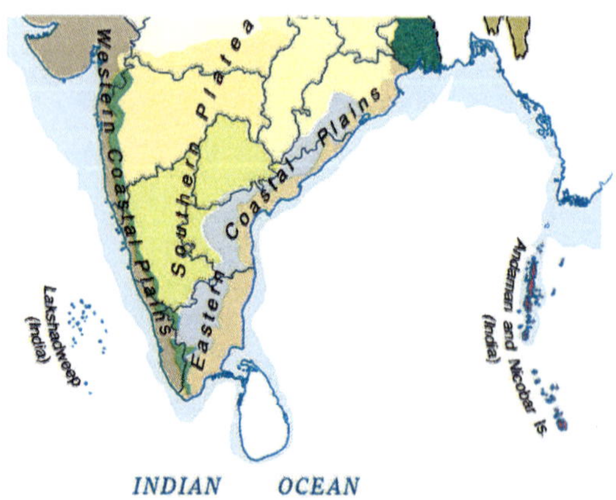

17 Pollution and Its Impact

Let's learn about...

- pollution.
- the types of pollution.
- the causes of pollution.
- the effects of pollution.
- prevention of pollution.

Key Terms

- contamination
- air pollution
- noise pollution
- water pollution
- acid rain
- pollutants
- soil pollution
- stagnant water
- prevention
- reduce
- reuse
- recycle

Reflect

Look at these pictures and write a sentence about each picture, describing what is happening.

....

....

....

....

....

....

Pollution is anything that makes the Earth dirty and unhealthy. It means the contamination of air, water, soil and the environment. The things that pollute the environment, like smoke, fumes, factory wastes and chemicals, are called pollutants. A person or an agent that causes pollution is a pollutant.

Pollution can be natural or human-made. Volcanic eruptions, dust storms and wildfires are some examples of natural pollution. Smoke from factories, throwing garbage into rivers and other water bodies, playing loud music during late hours are some of the sources of human-made pollution. There are four kinds of pollution—air, water, soil and noise pollution.

contamination: making a substance dirty or impure

Air Pollution

Air pollution

Air surrounds the Earth. It makes up the atmosphere. You know the atmosphere is made up of various kinds of gases such as oxygen, nitrogen, carbon dioxide, methane, water vapour and ozone. These gases exist in a definite balance in the atmosphere. An imbalance in the quantity of these gases causes air pollution. Smoke, dust and harmful emissions are the main sources of air pollution.

The following are the different sources of air pollution:

Sources of Air Pollution

- Black smoke from vehicles due to burning of fuel
- Smoke from burning stubble, wood and garden waste
- Smoke from burning coal and kerosene for domestic cooking and industrial use
- Release of harmful chemicals from factories
- Emission of poisonous gases from power plants, oil refineries and industries
- Dust from clearing land and cutting down trees
- Dust rising from construction activity

Effects of air pollution

Air pollution is very harmful for the health of living beings as people develop breathing problems. Animals and plants also get affected when the air is polluted as the temperature of that place rises, affecting the climate. One of the major effects of air pollution is acid rain. When air mixes with poisonous substances, it comes down as acid rain, which harms forests, water bodies, soil and buildings. Air pollution thins down the ozone layer that protects us from the harmful rays of the Sun.

FactPedia

We breathe in 20,000 litres of air everyday. This means that the more we breathe in polluted air, more dangerous chemicals enter our bodies.

Figure Out

What is smog?

Prevention of air pollution

Governments all around the world are encouraging the use of cleaner sources of energy, like windmills, hydroelectricity plants and solar energy, which do not cause any pollution. Laws are being made to make factories and industries more responsible about the pollutants they release. All vehicle owners have to get regular pollution checks for their vehicles. Car manufacturers are designing vehicles which are more energy efficient and cause less pollution. Diesel and petrol are being replaced by Compressed Natural Gas (CNG) as fuel, as it does not give out fumes. To reduce air pollution we can:

- walk short distances.
- use car pools.
- limit the use of air conditioners in our homes.
- Recycle and reuse things.
- plant more trees.

Green Earth

The government has set up different pollution control boards to monitor pollution and issue guidelines. National Green Tribunal has been set up to check and control the polluting bodies.

Air Pollution in NCT of Delhi

The National Capital Territory of Delhi is often cited as one of the most polluted city in the world due to severe air pollution. In November 2019, a thick cloud of smog engulfed the entire region. The smog was so thick that the visibility became very poor and flights could not take off or land. The schools had to be shut down in Delhi and the NCR region as the severe pollution was causing serious breathing problems for children and adults. People had to remain indoors. The farmers in northern India burn the stubble of their crops in the fields in the months of October and November each year. The rising smoke in combination with wind causes smog in adjoining areas but it became more severe due to vehicular pollution and delayed rains.

Water Pollution

Water is a precious resource without which life on the Earth cannot exist. Water pollution occurs when pollutants are released into water bodies, such as lakes, rivers and seas, directly or indirectly. Water pollution is harmful for plants, animals and human beings. Water becomes dirty when harmful pollutants mix with water sources. Standing water, which gets collected in and around the houses is known as stagnant water.

Water pollution

stubble: stem left in the field after harvesting crop

Sources of water pollution

- industrial waste
- fertilizers from fields
- Bathing of human beings and animals in the water bodies
- chemicals from factories
- untreated sewage from drains
- dumped household garbage
- construction waste material
- clothes cleaning agents like detergents
- oil spills

Water Pollution in Bengaluru

Bengaluru city is known for its lakes. The lake water is treated to supply drinking water in many parts of the city. Last few years have seen an increase in the levels of water pollution in Bengaluru. In 2019, Lakes Bellandur and Varthur had become frothy and Ulsoor lake turned into a fish graveyard. People fell sick after drinking contaminated water. Many industries continue to discharge untreated water into these lakes. The sewage from households also drains into these lakes.

Efforts are being made by the state government, National Green Tribunal and various NGOs to clean up these lakes.

Effects of water pollution

Ocean pollution

Water pollution is harmful for all living beings. Birds, such as seagulls and other aquatic animals, die because of water pollution. When humans consume fish and other seafood from a contaminated water body, it leads to illness and diseases. Drinking water that is polluted causes water-borne diseases, such as dysentery, jaundice and diarrhoea. Stagnant water breeds mosquitoes and can cause diseases like malaria and dengue.

Prevention of water pollution

To prevent and control water pollution, the first and foremost rule is not to throw garbage into water bodies. The government has made laws to ensure that industries treat the waste before releasing it into water bodies. Sewage must be treated before it is released into water bodies. Environment-friendly cleaning liquids must be used by

sewage: used water and waste substances that are produced by human bodies

all. Fertilizers and pesticides used in agriculture or gardening often seep through the soil into the groundwater, polluting it. Therefore, its usage must be minimal. We must not pollute the water in rivers or ponds by bathing or washing our clothes in them. Awareness must be created about keeping our water bodies clean.

Soil Pollution

Soil pollution occurs when we do not dispose off waste properly or we throw a lot of chemicals in the form of pesticides and fertilizers into the soil. Plastic containers, plastic bags, bottles, cans and glass do not decay and mix with the soil. They pile up in landfills where they are usually dumped.

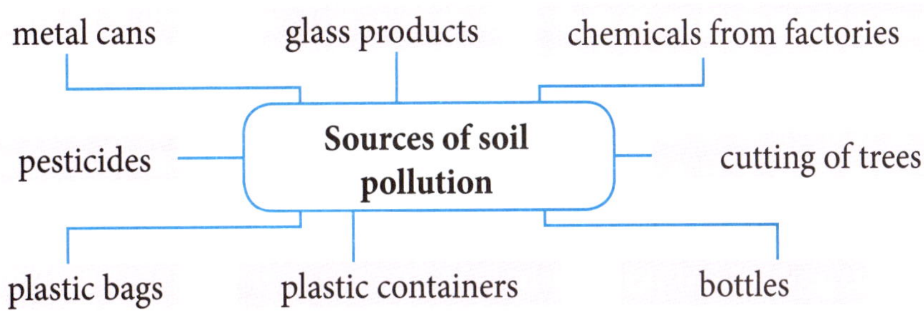

Effects of soil pollution

If the soil gets polluted, it affects all living beings. Pollution in soil harms the crops and plants, which may not allow them to survive. The dust of the polluted soil, if inhaled by people and animals, can cause respiratory diseases. Fruits and vegetables grown in polluted soil may cause illnesses. Garbage dumps breed rats and insects that spreads bad odour and diseases.

Soil pollution

Prevention of soil pollution

One way to prevent soil pollution is to start disposing waste properly. We must try to reduce, reuse and recycle waste. We should also reduce the use of products made up of plastic and synthetic materials. We should try to reuse old things to reduce the amount of waste produced. One can also recycle used objects and plastic to create new articles. Planting trees is another way to conserve the soil. Roots of grass, small plants and trees hold the soil firmly, stopping it from being washed away by rain or wind. We should try to spread awareness about the harmful effects of soil pollution.

pesticides: a chemical used for killing harmful insects in crops

Noise Pollution

A traffic jam

Noise pollution is caused when the sound produced causes discomfort to our ears. There are many things that increase the level of noise and cause noise pollution.

Sources of noise pollution

- Fireworks
- Shouting
- Construction Machines
- Traffic
- Aeroplanes
- Barking dogs
- Loud music
- Household gadgets
- Loud speakers

Effects of noise pollution

Unwanted noise causes irritation, sleep disturbance and a loss of hearing. It also disrupts our daily lives by spoiling the quality of our environment. Loud noise, such as bursting crackers, scares animals and birds. Too much noise may lead to stress and anxiety, headache and high blood pressure.

Noise prevention and control

Blowing horns unnecessarily is one of the most common causes of noise pollution. This is being regulated by the authorities. The use of loud speakers and loud music should be controlled. One must not put on loud music as it is likely to disturb the neighbourhood. Schools, colleges, and hospitals should be silence zones. Planting trees in industrial areas can absorb the loud noise.

DIY

Label the type of pollution that is being shown in the pictures below and name the pollutant.

....

....

....

....

....

....

....

....

In a Nutshell

- Pollution is anything that makes the environment dirty.
- There are four kinds of pollution—air, water, soil and noise.
- Air and water pollution cause diseases and loss of aquatic life.
- Soil pollution occurs when we do not dispose waste properly.
- Noise pollution is caused when the sound produced causes discomfort to the ears.
- We should prevent pollution of the Earth.

Workout

A. Fill in the blanks.

1. Smoke causes ....
2. Drinking polluted water can cause ....
3. Noise pollution can lead to .... problems.
4. We can conserve soil by.............................. .

B. Answer in one word.

1. The things that pollute the environment are called: ....
2. A chemical used for killing harmful insects in crops: ....
3. Contamination of the environment: ....
4. Liquid waste from factories: ....

C. Match the following.

	Column A		Column B
1.	smoke	a.	water pollution
2.	sewage	b.	soil pollution
3.	loudspeaker	c.	air pollution
4.	plastic bag	d.	noise pollution

D. Answer these questions in brief

1. Name two sources of pollution.
2. What are silence zones?
3. What is the full form of CNG ?
4. What causes soil or land pollution?

E. Answer these questions in detail.

1. Name three ways in which we can prevent and check air pollution.

2. Suggest three ways in which we can prevent and control water pollution.
3. What is the impact of noise pollution on human beings and animals?

Think Box

Why do you think industries or manufacturing units are not allowed to be set up near historical monuments?

Picture Study

Look at the picture and answer the questions.

1. What type of pollution does this picture show?
2. How will it affect the environment?
3. What measure can be taken to prevent it?

Life Skills and Values

Take a walk around your neighbourhood. Find out the types of pollutants you see in the area. Discuss an action plan with your neighbourhood friends on how to reduce the amount of waste generated.

Enjoy

A. Write a letter to the editor of a local newspaper sharing your concern about the pollution in your area. Suggest measures to reduce or control the pollution.

B. Divide yourselves into four groups. Make four charts on the four types of pollution, mentioning the causes, effects and prevention of pollution. Put it up in your corridor or class soft boards.

Weblinks

For more information, visit
https://kids.nationalgeographic.com/explore/nature/kids-vs-plastic/pollution/
https://kids.nationalgeographic.com/explore/nature/save-the-earth-hub/13-ways-to-save-the-earth-from-pollution/
Last accessed on 31/July/2020

18 Waste Management

Let's learn about...

- the types of waste.
- waste management.
- the effects of poor waste management.
- the ways to conserve our environment.

Key Terms

- conservation
- reusing
- recycling
- biodegradable
- waste management
- composting
- landfills
- non-biodegradable

Reflect

In a day-boarding school, 3000 children are served drinks in paper cups daily. These cups are thrown into the garbage bins. How do you think this affects our environment?

In the previous chapter, we learnt that human action has led to pollution. It also leads to wasting away of natural resources, like land, water and air. If we continue to pollute the Earth and use the natural resources unreasonably, the Earth would no longer be able to sustain life. We need to protect our natural environment which includes plants, animals, their habitats and our natural resources. The protection of the natural environment is called conservation.

Figure Out

What is rainwater harvesting?

A lot of waste is generated in our homes, offices, schools, farms, industries and hospitals every day. Where does the trash go? Mostly, it goes to a dump or a landfill. Waste material may range from a small chocolate wrapper to a large, old truck.

Types of Waste

The different types of waste are:

- liquid—sewage water from homes
- solid—paper, wood, metal, glass, cardboard
- hazardous—chemical batteries

FactPedia

Untreated wastewater has to be treated in factories with the help of chemicals to make it clean again.

sustain: to hold up under or withstand

- organic—food, peels, plants
- recyclable—paper, aluminum cans, glass
- construction and demolition—concrete, plastic, metal, wood, etc.
- e-waste—gadgets, old television sets, computers, etc.
- medical—bandages, syringes, needles, medicines

We need to dispose the garbage that we create responsibly and use our natural resources carefully, so that we can conserve our environment.

Waste Management

Waste management means collection, transportation, processing or disposal, managing and monitoring of waste material in a safe manner. There are two kinds of waste—biodegradable and non-biodegradable. Biodegradable waste comes from plants and animals. It mixes with the soil without harming our environment. Food items like vegetables, fruits and paper, are biodegradable waste. Non-biodegradable waste, such as plastic, tin, aluminum, thermocol® and glass, cause harm to the environment as they do not mix with the soil. Waste must be sorted into biodegradable and non-biodegradable, before being disposed.

Waste management

How is waste managed?

Burning: When waste is burnt, it creates a lot of carbon dioxide. Countries like Denmark and Germany have machines that burn, process and manage the waste.

Landfills: The waste is taken to a place where it is dumped. It may or may not have been sorted before being put here.

Composting: All the biodegradable items, such as peels of vegetables and fruits, leaves, twigs and flowers, decay. This decayed organic matter makes good manure or humus. Kitchen and garbage waste can be collected in a pit, or a box with small holes, and allowed to decay for some time and then used as manure.

Composting

Reducing: Reducing is simply cutting down on the waste that we make. For instance, we can avoid wastage of food by not taking too much food on our plate, by not wasting paper, water, electricity etc.

Reusing: Things that we do not need can be given to others who may find them more useful. For example, old clothes, toys, books, jars, boxes and bottles.

decay: the process of being destroyed by natural causes

Recycling: It is the method by which waste material, such as plastic, paper, glass, tin, cans and aluminum, can be made into new, useful products. Recycling protects the environment, conserves natural resources and saves energy.

Various government agencies, local government, non-governmental organisations are working for waste management.

Doing Our Bit

We can follow the steps given here to make sure that we conserve the environment:

> **Green Earth**
>
> We should dig compost pits where we can throw all the biodegradable wastes that we use.

- Create less waste by reducing the consumption of paper, fuel, water etc.
- Use crockery at home that can be washed and reused.
- Reuse things like gift wrapping paper, packing boxes, clothing, furniture and toys.
- Recycle by changing the original look and shape of things such that all these things continue to be useful and are not required to be thrown away.
- For instance, it can be done by, using an old tyre as a swing, converting old bottles into useful storage jars and writing on both sides of a sheet of paper.
- Reuse old, and pots and other containers to grow plants.
- Dispose off waste only in designated dustbins and trash cans.

DIY

Let's recycle! Learn how to make your own handmade paper.

- Collect scraps of used paper and cut them into pieces.
- Soak them in a bowl of water overnight.
- With the help of an adult, blend the soaked paper into a gooey paste.

- Next, take the wire mesh, keep it over a tray and put the paste over it.
- Keep pressing to flatten it, and spread it on the mesh with something flat, like a pencil box etc. This makes the water from the paste to go down the mesh.
- Then, take some dried flowers and place them on the wet surface of the paste, lightly pressing them into the paste.
- Leave it to dry for the night.
- In the morning, you will find that your handmade paper is ready!

Conservation of the environment

Taking care of our environment is important for the survival and health of human beings, plants and animals. Conservation of our environment and our natural resources means prevention of loss, wastage, damage and destruction of our environment. Conserving the environment is a collective effort and we all need to do our bit.

Keeping the environment clean

In a Nutshell

- We must conserve the environment and its natural resources.
- The different kinds of waste are solid, liquid, chemical, medical, organic and e-waste.
- Waste management is the collection, transportation, processing and disposal of waste in a safe manner.
- Waste can be biodegradable and non-biodegradable.
- Waste can be disposed by burning, being put in landfills, recycling, reducing, reusing and composting.
- Various government agencies, local government, non-governmental organisations are also working for waste management.

Workout

A. Fill in the blanks.

1. We need to protect or .... our environment.
2. Pollution leads to environmental ....
3. Plants and animal waste is ....
4. We need to .... garbage very responsibly.

B. Match the columns.

	Column A		Column B
1.	e-waste	a.	food, vegetables and plants
2.	medical	b.	glass, aluminum, cans
3.	hazardous	c.	sewage
4.	solid	d.	bandages, syringes
5.	liquid	e.	batteries, chemicals
6.	organic	f.	old electrical gadgets

C. Write T for true and F for false.

1. Waste must be sorted out before it is disposed. ☐
2. Proper waste management conserves our environment. ☐
3. Only the government is responsible for the conservation of the resources. ☐
4. A lot of waste is produced by human activities. ☐

D. Answer these questions in brief.

1. What is the difference between biodegradable and non-biodegradable waste?
2. Why is burning of waste not a good method of waste disposal?
3. What is composting?
4. Who helps to conserve the environment?

E. Answer these questions in detail.

1. What is environmental conservation?
2. Define waste management.
3. What are the different ways in which waste is managed?
4. Name the different ways in which we can conserve our environment.

Think Box

Human action is the main cause for environmental pollution. But, only human action can save the environment. Write three things that you can do to prevent environmental pollution.

....

Picture Study

Look at the picture and answer the questions.

1. What is this area called?
2. Where do you think it is located?
3. What is it made up of?

Life Skills and Values

Make a weekly record of the waste generated from your house. List three ways in which you can reduce or reuse the following waste–food, water, paper, electronic waste.

Enjoy

Make planters from waste

Take some old bottles.

Cut a bottle into half and punch small holes into it. Place a plant or a sapling in it.

Hang these bottles in the garden or balcony, and your wall garden is ready.

Weblinks

For more information, visit
https://kids.nationalgeographic.com/explore/celebrations/earth-day/
https://kids.nationalgeographic.com/explore/nature/reduce-your-waste/
Last accessed on 31/July/2020

Across the Boundary 4

It All Adds Up

- Kiki, her mother, and her father shower daily. Each shower uses 40 litres of water.
- How many litres of water does the family use to bathe every day? ....
- How many litres of water does the family use to bathe each week?................................

Spelling Bee

How good are your spelling skills? Circle the wrong spellings in the sentences below and write the correct spellings in the blanks given.

1. Saving enregy is as easy as A-B-C. ....
2. Use soler enegry by letting the sun inside in winter. ....
3. We should resycle old things. ....
4. Smok from factories pollutes the air. ....
5. Reduse your engery use by turning off the lights when you leave the room ....

Taking Responsibility

Tick the sentences which you feel are your responsibilities.

1. Cleaning your room ☐
2. Taking care of your pet ☐
3. Washing your own clothes ☐
4. Keeping your surroundings clean ☐
5. Littering the classroom ☐
6. Driving yourself to school ☐
7. Caring for the environment ☐
8. Watering the plants ☐

Snap Recap

The Snap Recap section contains a collection of mind maps that draw the outline of the concepts of you have learned in this book. These are also called concept maps or graphic organizers. Mind mapping is a useful technique that helps you learn more effectively and improves the way that you record information. They help you see the way pieces of information fit together. Mind maps also help you remember information, as they hold it in a format that your mind finds easy to recall.

Understanding History

- Periods
  - Ancient
  - Medieval
  - Modern
- Sources
  - Archaeological
    - Monuments
    - Coins
    - Inscriptions
  - Literary
    - Religious texts
    - Non-religious texts
    - Biographies
    - Autobiographies

Calendar

- Gregorian
  - Most commonly used calendar
  - Has twelve months
  - January is the first month
  - Eleven months have 30 or 31 days
  - February has 28 or 29 days
  - Leap year has 366 days
- Saka
  - Indian national calendar
  - Has twelve months
  - Chaitra is the first month
  - Eleven months have 30 or 31 days
  - February has 28 or 29 days
  - Leap year has 366 days
  - Starts 78 years after Gregorian

Responsibilities of a Good Citizen

- ✓ Respecting neighbours and all citizens
- ✓ Obeying traffic rules

- ✓ Participating in elections

- ✓ Caring for Public Property
- ✓ Not littering
- ✓ Using water and electricity carefully

Domains of the Earth

Lithosphere
- The solid surface of the Earth
- Made up of soil, rocks and other solid particles
- Called the crust

Hydrosphere
- All the water bodies found on the surface of the Earth
- Supports life on Earth
- Controls Earth's favourable climate

Atmosphere
- The layer of air surrounding the Earth
- Protects the Earth from the Sun's harmful rays
- Made up of several gases

Biosphere
- Made up of the parts of the Earth where life exists.
- Includes lithosphere, hydrosphere and atmosphere
- Has many ecosystems

Motions of the Earth

Rotation

- The spinning of the Earth on its axis
- The Earth takes 24 hours to complete one rotation.
- Rotation causes day and night.

Revolution

- The movement of the Earth around the Sun in its orbit
- The Earth takes 365 1/4 days to complete one revolution.
- Revolution causes seasons.

Major Landforms of the Earth

Mountains
The highest landform on the Earth

Islands
A piece of land surrounded by water on all sides.

Hills
High landforms that are lower than the mountains

Deserts
- Large areas of barren land
- Can be hot or cold

Valley
A low area between two mountains or hills

Isthmus
A narrow strip of land that joins two large bodies of land

Plateau
A highland that is flat on the top like a table

Plains
Large regions of flatland

Water Bodies

Sea
A large area of water but not as big as an ocean.

Oceans
A large and deep area of water.
- Pacific
- Atlantic
- Indian
- Arctic
- Antarctic

River
A body of freshwater flowing across the land.
- Snow fed rivers
- Rain fed rivers

Lake
A body of water surrounded by land on all sides

Strait
A narrow channel of sea joining two larger expanses of water.

Bay
A large body of water connected to an ocean or sea by an inlet of land.

Maps

Types

Physical
Shows the physical features such as mountains, hills, rivers and lakes.

Political
Shows the natural boundary, states of a country, location of cities, capital cities.

Thematic Maps
- Road maps
- Climatic maps
- Tourist Maps

Features
- Scale
- Symbols
- Colours

States of India

Capital: New Delhi

- **28 States**
  - headed by a Chief Minister
- **8 Union Territories**
  - directly ruled by the Central Government
- **Neighbours**
  - Nepal
  - Bhutan
  - Pakistan
  - Bangladesh
  - Afghanistan
  - Sri Lanka
  - Myanmar
  - China
  - Maldives

India—Physical Divisions

The Northern Mountains

Himalayas

- Himadri
- Himachal
- Shiwalik

The Desert Region

Thar Desert

The Coastal Regions

- Eastern Ghat is wider
- Western Ghat is narrower

The Northern Plains

Ganga, Yamuna, Indus, Sutlej flow through this plain

The Islands

- Andaman and Nicobar in Bay of Bengal
- Lakshadweep in the Arabian Sea

The Peninsula Plateau

- Malwa
- Chota Nagpur
- Deccan

Features of Physical Divisions

Himalayas

- Cold and cool windy climate
- Natural barrier prevents the cold winds
- Stops the rain bearing monsoon winds
- Source of snow-fed rivers
- Rich variety of vegetation

Plains

- Hot in summer and cold in winters
- Rich fertile alluvial soil, good for crops
- Receives rainfall for rain-fed rivers
- Rivers are navigable
- Flat area promotes agriculture and trade
- Thickly populated cities

Deserts

- Very hot and dry
- Scanty rainfall
- Sparse vegetation
- Sandy soil

Plateaus

- Black soil good for growing cotton & pulses
- The storehouse of minerals
- Provides raw material for industries.
- Largest coal producing belt in India
- Dams on rivers produce hydroelectricity

Major Rivers of India

Perennial or Snow fed

- Ganga
- Yamuna
- Kaveri
- Chambal
- Sutlej
- Ravi
- Jhelum
- Krishna
- Godavari
- Pennar

Non-perennial or seasonal

- Tapi
- Narmada

The Northern Mountains

Uttarakhand
- Capital: Dehradun
- Places of interest: Mussorie, Badrinath
- Rivers: Ganga & Yamuna
- Vegetation: sal, teak, rhodendron, orchards

Jammu & Kashmir UT
- Capital: Srinagar (S) & Jammu (W)
- Places of interest: Gulmarg, Pahalgaon
- Rivers: Indus, Jhelum & Sutlej
- Vegetation: cedar, pine trees

Ladakh UT
- Capital: Leh
- Places of interest: Leh and Kargil
- Rivers: Indus & Zanskar
- Vegetation: sparse

Himachal Pradesh
- Capital: Shimla
- Places of interest: Manali, Kullu
- Rivers: Beas, Jhelum & Sutlej
- Vegetation: orchards, deodar, pine trees

The Northeastern States

Assam
- Capital: Dispur
- River: Brahmaputra
- Gateway to the northeast
- Places of interest: Kaziranga National park, Kamakhaya Temple

Arunachal Pradesh
- Capital: Itanagar
- River: Brahmaputra
- Places of interest: Twang Monastery, Namdapha National Park

Manipur
- Capital: Imphal
- Land of the classical Manipuri dance
- Places of interest: Loktak lake

Nagaland
- Capital: Kohima
- Places of interest: Naga hills

Meghalaya
- Capital: Shillong
- Land of the Khasi, Garo and Jaintia Hills
- Places of interest: Mawsynram, Nohkalikai waterfall

Tripura
- Capital: Agartala
- Places of interest: Ujjayanta Palace

Mizoram
- Capital: Aizwal
- Cheraw, a popular folk dance

Sikkim
- Capital: Gangtok
- River: Brahmaputra

Northern Plains

Punjab
- Capital: Chandigarh
- Rivers: Ravi, Sutlej, Beas
- Places of interest: Ludhiana, Golden Temple in Amritsar, Jalandhar

Haryana
- Capital: Chandigarh
- Places of interest: Gurugram, Fardidabad, Ambala, Karnal

Delhi
- Capital: New Delhi: national capital
- Rivers: Yamuna
- Places of interest: Red Fort, Qutub Minar, Humayun's tomb

Uttar Pradesh
- Capital: Lucknow
- Rivers: Ganga, Yamuna, Gomti, Ghaghara, Betwa, Chambal
- Places of interest: Taj Mahal in Agra, Kanpur, Lucknow

Bihar
- Capital: Patna
- Rivers: Ganga, Gandak, Kosi, Son
- Places of interest: Bodh Gaya, Nalanda

West Bengal
- Capital: Kolkata
- Rivers: Hooghly
- Places of interest: Victoria Memorial, Botanical Gardens in Kolkata, Darjiling

Desert regions

Rajasthan
- Capital: Jaipur
- Rivers: Luni, Banas
- Places of interest: Jaisalmer, Jaipur, Udaipur, Bikaner

Gujarat
- Capital: Gandhinagar
- Rivers: Narmada, Tapi, Sabarmati
- Places of interest: Sabarmati Ashram Gir forests, Dwarka

The Peninsular Regions and the Islands

Madhya Pradesh
- Capital: Bhopal
- River: Narmada Betwa, Chambal, Son
- Places of interest: Gwalior, Indore, Jabalpur Panchmari, Kanha Tiger Reserve, Bandhavgarh National Park

Chhattisgarh
- Capital: Raipur
- River: Mahanadi, Indravati, Arpa, Pairi
- Places of interest: Bhilai

Jharkhand
- Capital: Ranchi
- River: Damodar, Subarnarekha, Brahmani, Son
- Places of interest: Dhanbad, Jamshedpur, Bokaro

Odisha
- Capital: Bhubaneswar
- River: Mahanadi
- Places of interest: Cuttack, Puri, Lake Chilka, Paradip port

Goa
- Capital: Panaji
- Places of interest: Marmagaon, Madgaon and beaches

Maharashtra
- Capital: Mumbai
- River: Godavari, Krishna
- Places of interest: Pune, Nasik, Mahabaleshwar, Panchgani

Andhra Pradesh and Telengana
- Capital: Hyderabad
- River: Krishna, Godavari
- Places of interest: Salarjung Museum, the Charminar, Faluknama Palace, Film City, Balaji Temple

Karnataka
- Capital: Bengaluru
- River: Krishna, Kaveri
- Places of interest: Mysore, Hampi, Belur

Kerala
- Capital: Thiruvananthapuram
- River: Periyar
- Places of interest: Guruvayur Temple, Cochin is a port town

Tamil Nadu
- Capital: Chennai
- River: Kaveri
- Places of interest: Madurai, Mahabalipuram, Thanjavur

The Island Region

Andaman and Nicobar

- Bay of Bengal
- Capital : Port Blair
- Places: Cellular jail

Lakshadweep

- Arabian Sea
- Capital : Kavaratti

The Diversity of India

- The Constitution of India mentions 22 scheduled languages.
- National, harvest and religious festivals are celebrated all over India.
- The people of India eat different kinds of food.
- Indians wear varied clothes in different regions according to the climate.
- There is unity in diversity

Pollution and its Impact

Air

Sources

- Buses, cars, vehicles
- Factories, power plants, industries, oil refineries
- The burning of wood, leaves, crops and coal or kerosene
- Clearing of forests

Water

Sources

- Industrial waste
- Fertilizers
- Bathing
- Cleaning
- Untreated sewage
- Garbage from homes
- Construction waste material

Soil

Sources

- Pesticides
- Metal cans
- Glass products
- Cutting trees
- Chemicals from factories
- Plastic bags and containers

Noise

Sources

- Car horns
- Aeroplanes
- Loud music
- Household gadgets
- Loud speakers
- Barking dogs
- Traffic
- Construction machines

Waste Management

Waste

Types

- Liquid
- Solid
- Hazardous
- Organic
- Recyclable
- Construction and demolition
- E-waste
- Medical

Kinds

- Biodegradable
- Non- Biodegradable

Management

Methods

- Burning
- Landfills
- Reusing
- Composting
- Recycling

Test Yourself 1

A. Choose the correct answer.

1. History helps us to know about our ....
   a. past b. present c. future
2. The Saka calendar is behind the Gregorian calendar by .... years.
   a. 12 b. 76 c. 78
3. The surface of the Earth on which we live is called the ....
   a. lithosphere b. biosphere c. hydrosphere
4. The most populated continent in the world is ....
   a. Europe b. Asia c. America
5. The .... is a rain-fed river.
   a. Ganga b. Yamuna c. Narmada
6. A process by which people choose their leaders is called ....
   a. election b. nomination c. oration
7. We can locate cities on a ....
   a. physical map b. political map c. road map

B. Fill in the blanks.

1. .... are remains of ancient plants and animals.
2. .... is a subject that teaches us how the government of a country works.
3. Every voter in India has a special identity card known as the ....
4. When the southern hemisphere is tilted away from the Sun, it has .... season.
5. The .... is the hottest part of the Earth.
6. An .... is a narrow strip of land that joins two large bodies of water.

C. Name the following.

1. An account written by a ruler himself: ....
2. A person belonging to a country: ....
3. The island continent: ....
4. The process by which water changes its form on the Earth: ....
5. The administrative head of a state: ....

D. Identify these pictures.

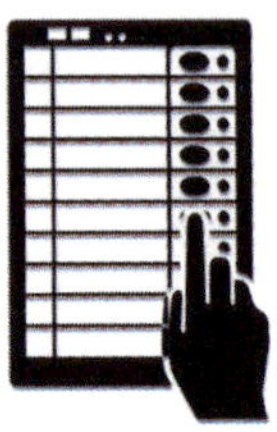

....

E. Explain the following.

1. It is important to study history.
2. It is the duty of every citizen to take care of public property.
3. Parks and monuments are public property.

F. Answer these questions in short.

1. Name the different periods of history.
2. Name the two types of sources of history.
3. Name the four major domains of the Earth.
4. Define a peninsula.
5. Why do we use symbols on a map?

G. Answer these questions in detail.

1. Write a short note on the archaeological sources of history.
2. List the responsibilities of a good citizen.
3. Describe in detail how the revolution of the Earth causes seasons.
4. Write a short note on Biosphere.
5. Name any six neighbouring countries of India.

H. Draw and label a neat diagram to show the revolution of the Earth.

Test Yourself II

A. Choose the correct answers.

1. India is divided into .... geographical divisions.
   a. 5 b. 6 c. 8
2. The .... act as a natural barrier on the north.
   a. Nilgiris b. Himalayas c. Satpura
3. The Khasi and Garo hills are located in ....
   a. Meghalaya b. Nagaland c. Assam
4. Gidda is a folk dance from ....
   a. Gujarat b. Punjab c. Bihar
5. Nagarjuna Dam is built on the river ....
   a. Krishna b. Kaveri c. Godavari
6. The Indian constitution recognizes .... languages.
   a. 22 b. 30 c. 18

B. Fill in the blanks.

1. A person or an agent that causes pollution is a ....
2. The river .... in India flows from east to west.
3. The .... islands are in the Arabian Sea.
4. River Ganga rises in the............................ .
5. .... is the folk dance of Assam.
6. .... is another name for the bamboo dance in Mizoram.

C. Name the following.

1. The highest mountain peak in the world: ....
2. A piece of land surrounded by water on three sides: ....
3. The winter capital of Jammu and Kashmir: ....
4. A distributary of the river Ganga: ....
5. Capital of Chhattisgarh: ....
6. The rainiest place in the world: ....

D. Write down the difference between the following.

1. Biodegradable and non-biodegradable wastes
2. Perennial and non-perennial rivers
3. Delta and estuary
4. Organic waste and e-waste
5. Recycling and composting

E. Answer these questions in brief.

1. Name two classical dances of India.
2. What is the staple food in the coastal areas of India?
3. Name two tourist attractions in Arunachal Pradesh.
4. What are the two ranges that separate the Deccan Plateau from the northern plains?
5. What is waste management?

F. Answer the following questions in details.

1. Write down the importance of the Himalayas for India.
2. What causes water pollution? Write two ways you can prevent water pollution.
3. Write a short note on Meghalaya.
4. Write different ways of waste management.
5. What steps can you take to conserve the environment?

G. Picture Study

Look at the pictures and answer the questions that follow.

1. What kind of pollution is being depicted in the picture?
2. What are the students doing? Why do they need to do this?

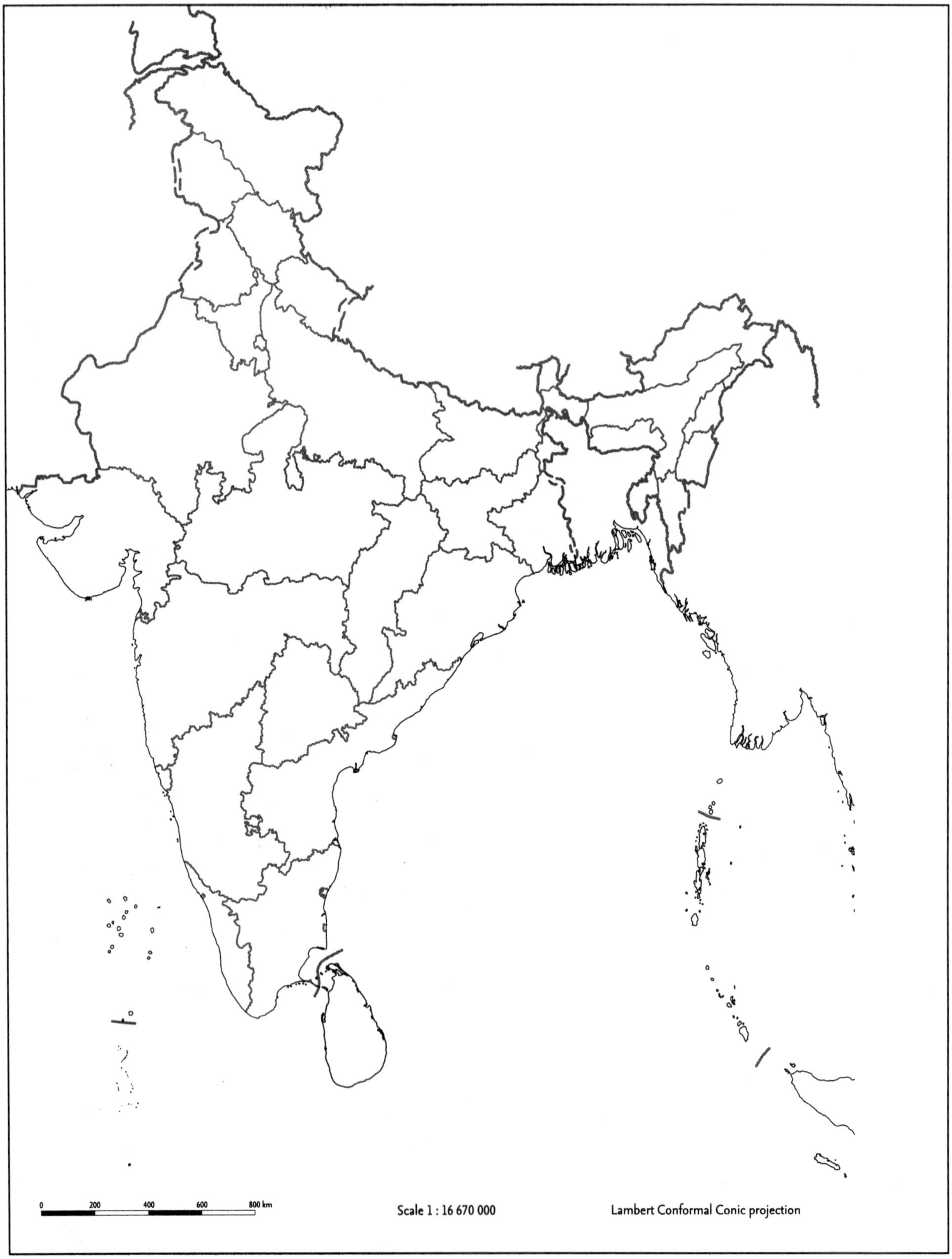

Political Map of India-Outline

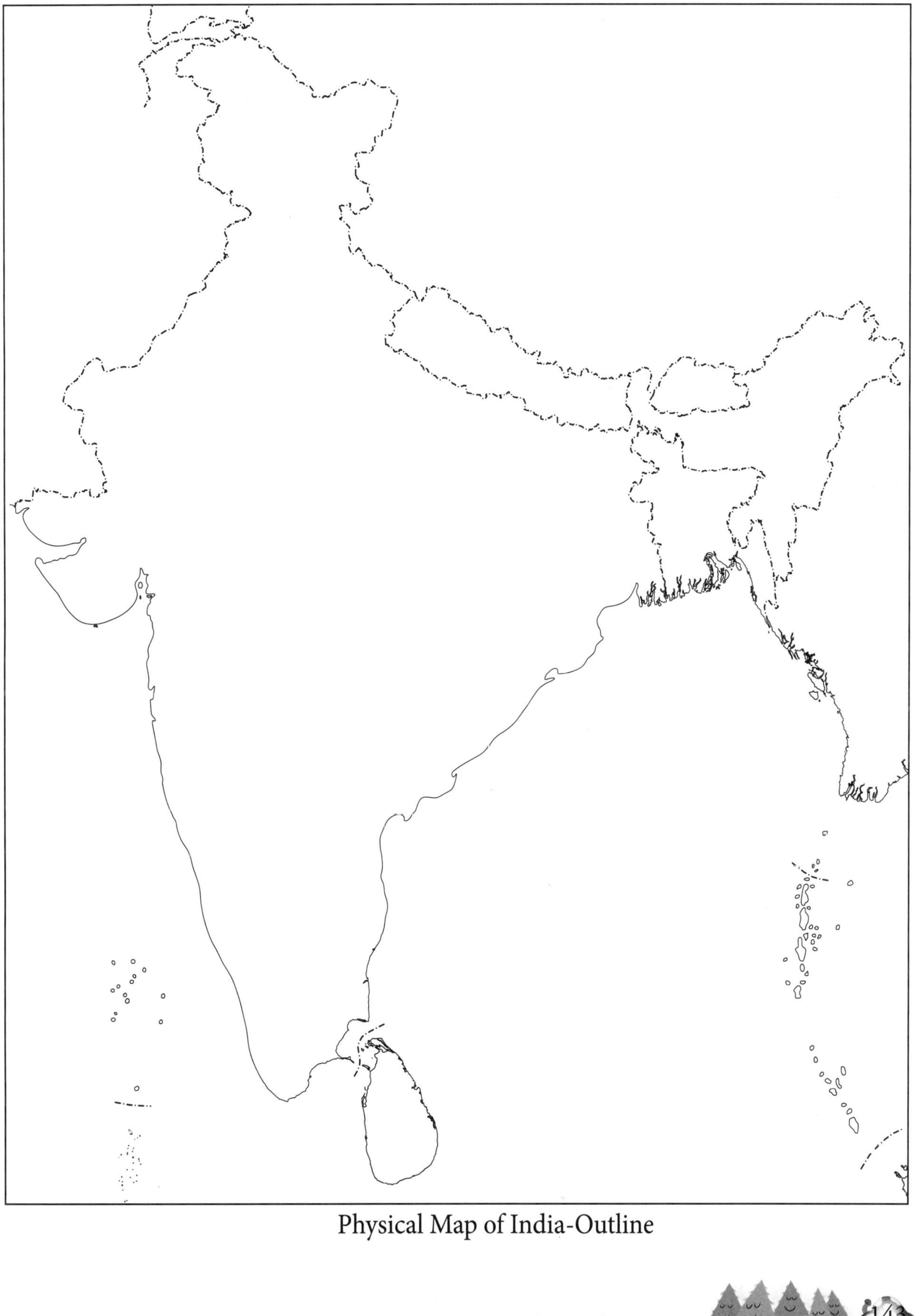

Physical Map of India-Outline

How well do you know your country? Name the states and their capitals.

GAME

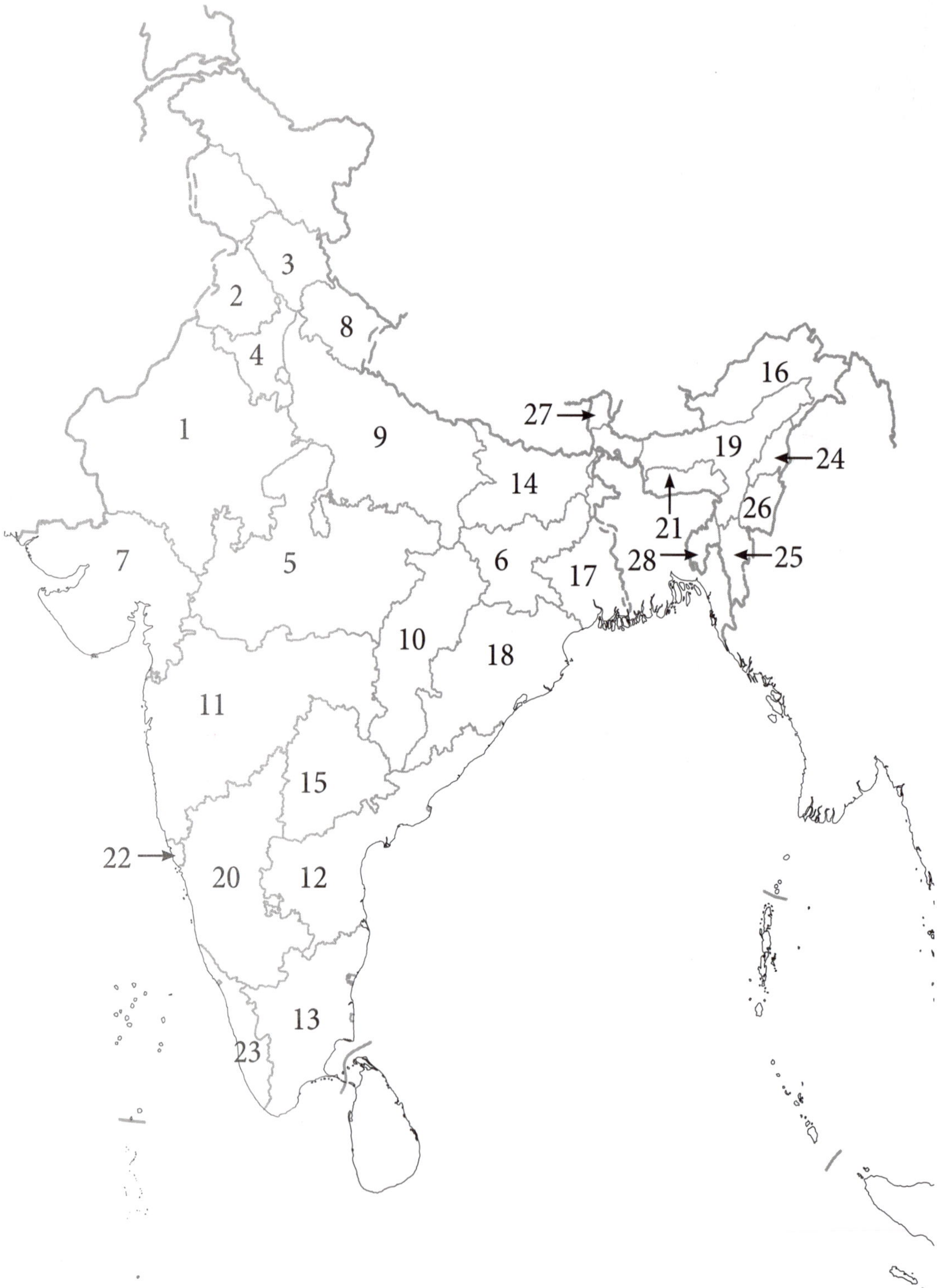

Write down the numbers 1 to 36 in chits of paper and put them in a bowl. Each player must take a chit. The player with the highest number starts the game by finding the corresponding number on the map and naming the state and the capital. If it is correct, you gain two points and if it is wrong, you do not get any point. Remember to check the answers and keep the score.